EAGLES ILLUSTRATED
Fighters of World War II

by Thomas A. Tullis

North American P-51D-10-NA

"PETIE 2nd" s/n:44-14151 • Lt. Col. John C. Meyer • 487th FS

Notes:
Meyer's score stood at 24 kills when WWII ended (20 shown).
The U.S. national insignia is the 'low visibility' type with Grey star and bars instead of White.
The swastikas and name "PETIE 2nd" were Yellow, not White as shown in other publications.
John Charles Meyer was enshrined into the National Aviation Hall of Fame in 1988.

Colors:
Overall natural metal
Prop Blades: Black with Yellow tips
Identification markings: Medium Blue forward fuselage and spinner

References:
Aces of the Eighth by Gene Stafford and William Hess. Squadron Signal Pub. 1973.
P-51 Mustang by Larry Davis. Squadron Signal Pub. 1995.

Focke-Wulf Fw 190 D-9

Oberstleutnant Gerhard Michalski • Stab./JG 4 • April 1945

Notes:
Forward cowl has had additional camouflage added (interpreted as a neutral Gray) over factory applied RLM 83.
Note the non-parallel edges of the RV bands.
The spelling of the pilot's name is correct, many publications have spelled it incorrectly as 'Michaelski'.

Colors:
Undersurfaces: RLM 76. Uppersurfaces: RLM 83, RLM 75 • Upperwing and stabilizer elevator: RLM 83, RLM 75
Spinner: Black with White Spiral • Prop Blades: RLM 70 Black Green
RV bands: Black/White/Black with Black/White pinstripes
Cowl: Additional field applied camouflage applied. See note above.

References:
Broken Eagles 1 Fw 190D by Carl Hildebrandt. Fighter Pictorials, 1987.
The Official Monogram Painting Guide to German Aircraft 1935-1945 by Ken Merrick & Thomas Hitchcock.
Monogram Aviation Pub., 1980.
Monogram Close-Up 10 Fw 190D by Richard Smith & Eddie Creek. Monogram Aviation Pub., 1986.

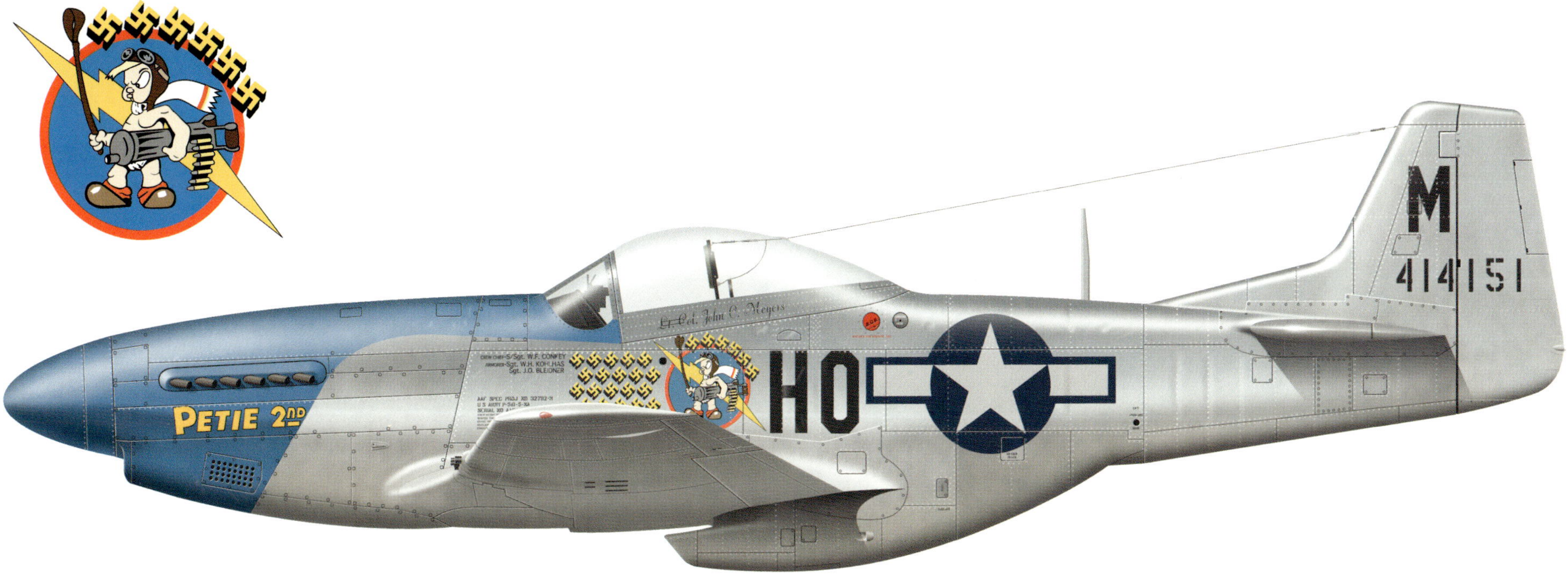
M
414151
PETIE 2ND
HO

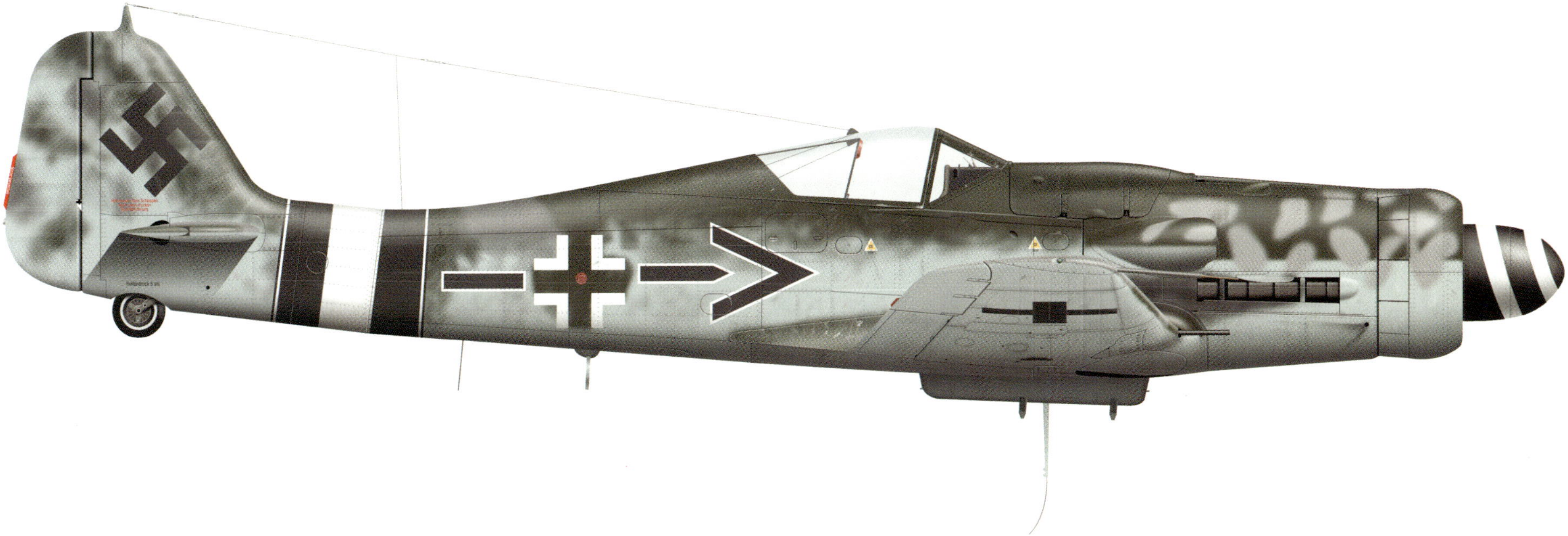

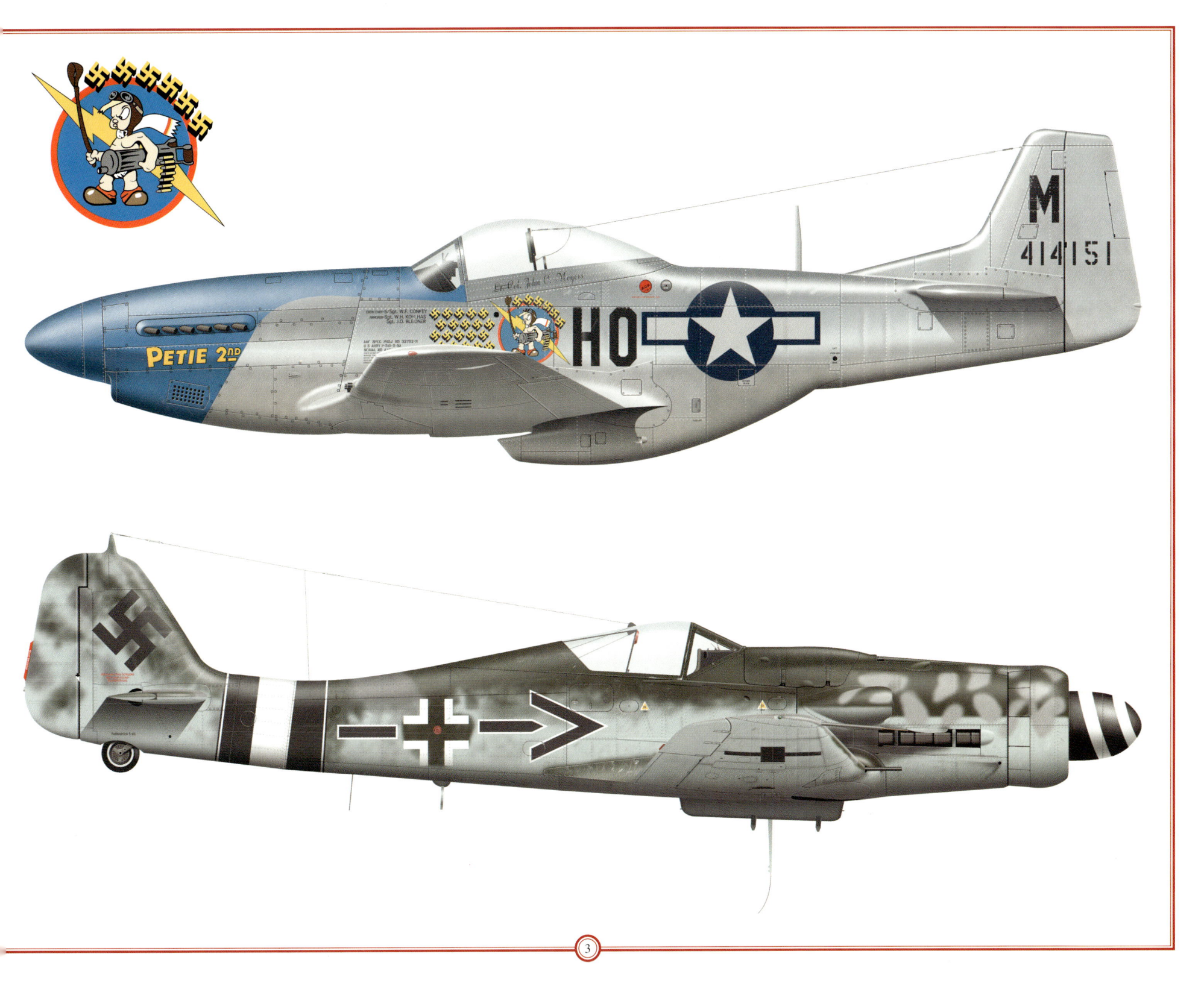

Focke-Wulf Fw 190 A-8

Maj. Walther Dahl • JG 300

Notes:
Previous fuselage markings have been over painted.
Badge on cowl was not used by JG 300 and was most likely applied for publicity purposes.
Some researchers believe that there was no blue background on the badge.

Colors:
Undersurfaces: RLM 76
Uppersurfaces: RLM 74, RLM 75
Upperwing and horizontal stabilizer: RLM 74, RLM 75
Spinner: Black with White Spiral • Propeller Blades: RLM 70

References:
Focke Wulf Jagdflugzeug Fw190A, Dora & Ta152 by Peter Rodeike.

Supermarine Spitfire Mk Vb

Robert Stanford-Tuck Wing • Biggin Hill Wing • January 1942

Notes:
Robert Stanford-Tuck was the Commander of the Biggin Hill Wing and had 29 kills.
On January 28, 1942, he was shot down by German ground fire. While attempting to glide down for a crash landing a German gun emplacement began firing on him. Stanford-Tuck was able to get off a short burst before crashing, placing a round down the barrel of the 20mm gun, splitting it wide open.

Colors:
Undersurfaces: Medium Sea Grey • Uppersurfaces: Ocean Grey, Dark Green
Spinner: Sky with Red tip • Prop blades: Black with Yellow tips

References:
Spitfire in action by Jerry Scutts. Squadron Signal Pub.
Spitfire-A Complete Fighting History by Alfred Price.

5

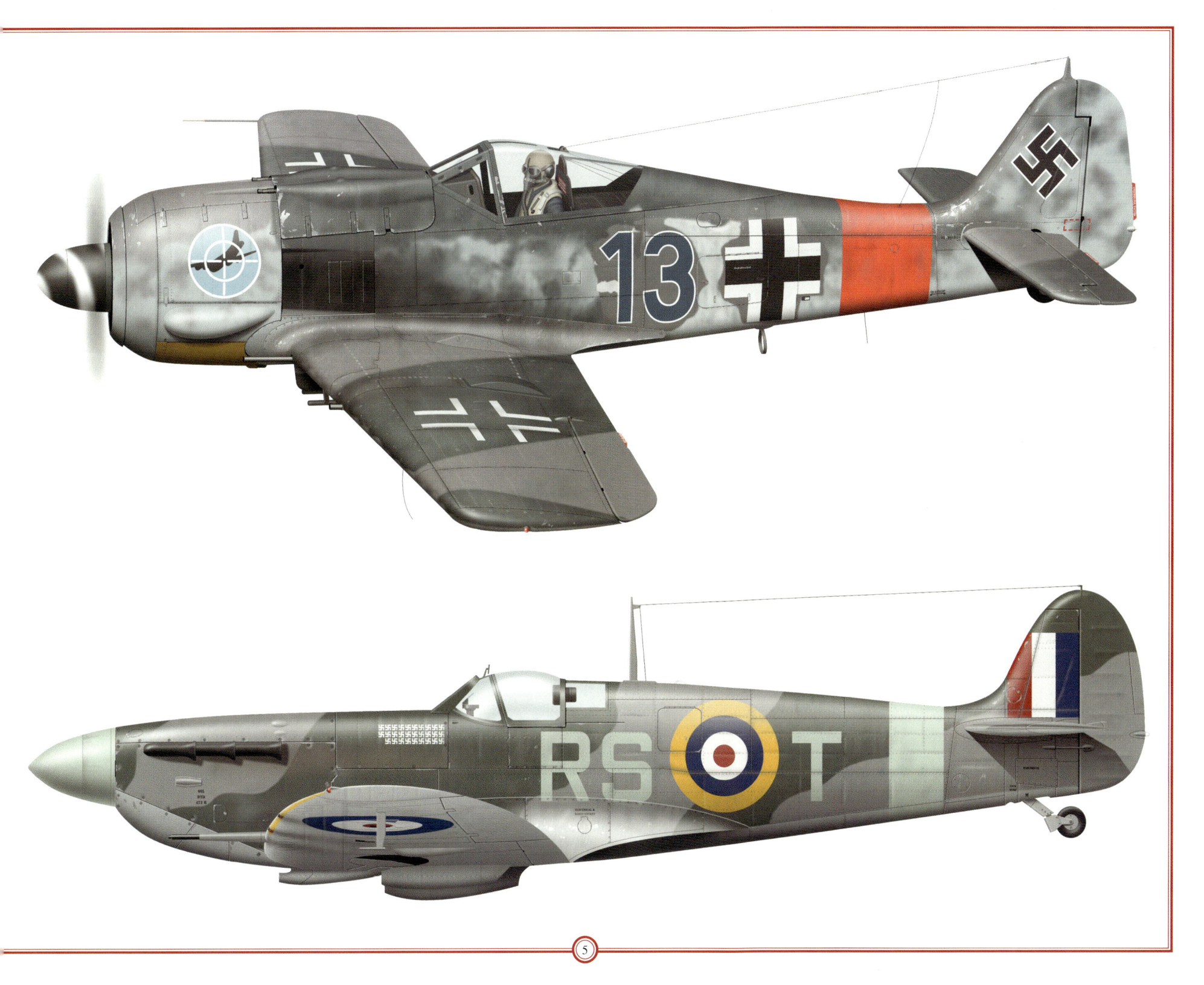

Messerschmitt Bf 109 G-6

W. Nr.: 440141 • Oblt. Wilhelm Schilling • 9./JG 54 • Feb. 1944

Colors:
Undersurfaces: RLM 76 • Uppersurfaces: RLM 74, RLM 75 with RLM 71 overspray
Spinner: Black with White spiral • Prop Blades: RLM 70

References:
Messerschmitt Bf 109 F, G, & K Series by J. Prien & P. Rodeike. Schiffer., 1993.

Focke-Wulf Fw 190 A-6

W. Nr.: Unknown   Pilot: Uffz. Kunze 1./JG 1   Date: 1943

Notes:
Note personal emblem "Friedel" under cockpit.
This aircraft had a replacement cowl in third Staffel colors.
ETC 501 centerline rack is unconfirmed

Colors:
Undersurfaces: RLM 76
Uppersurfaces: RLM 74, RLM 75
Upperwing and horizontal stabilizer: RLM 74, RLM 75
Spinner: White • Prop Blades: RLM 70

References:
JG 1 Historie de la Jagdgeschwader 1 "Oesau" by Eric Mombeek. Collection HISTOIRE DE L'AVIATION No 3, 1997.

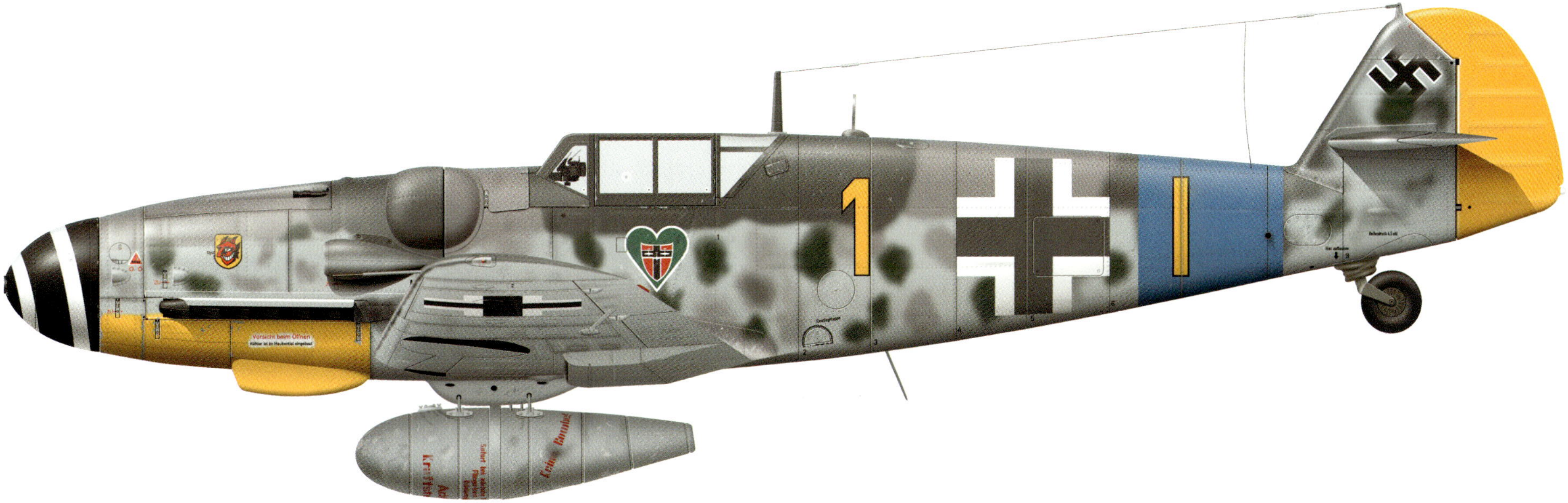

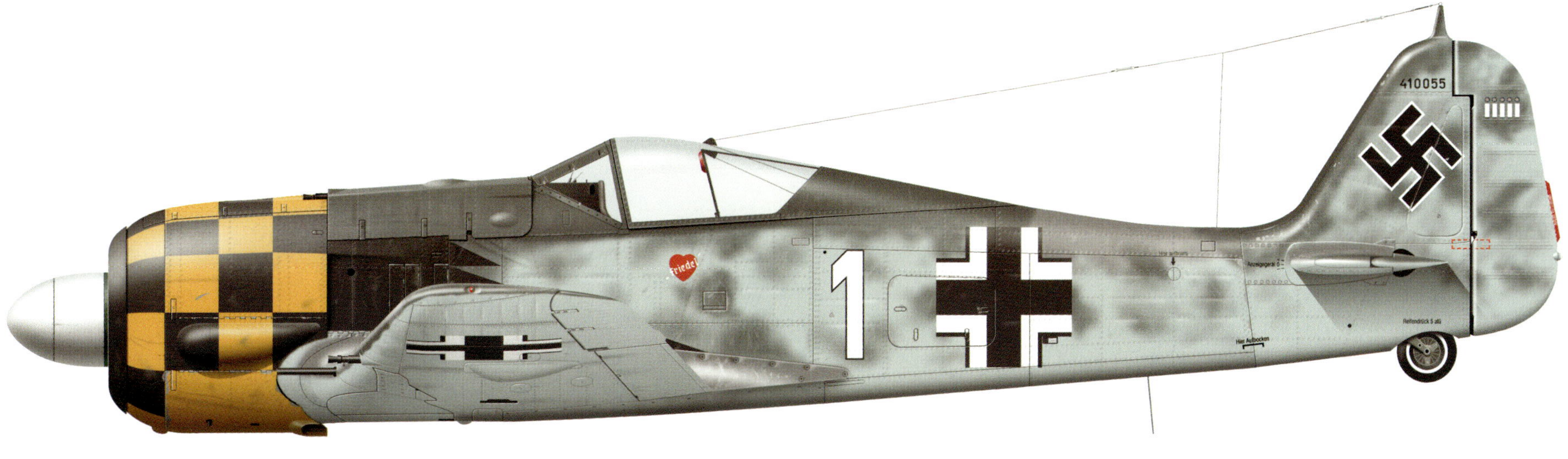

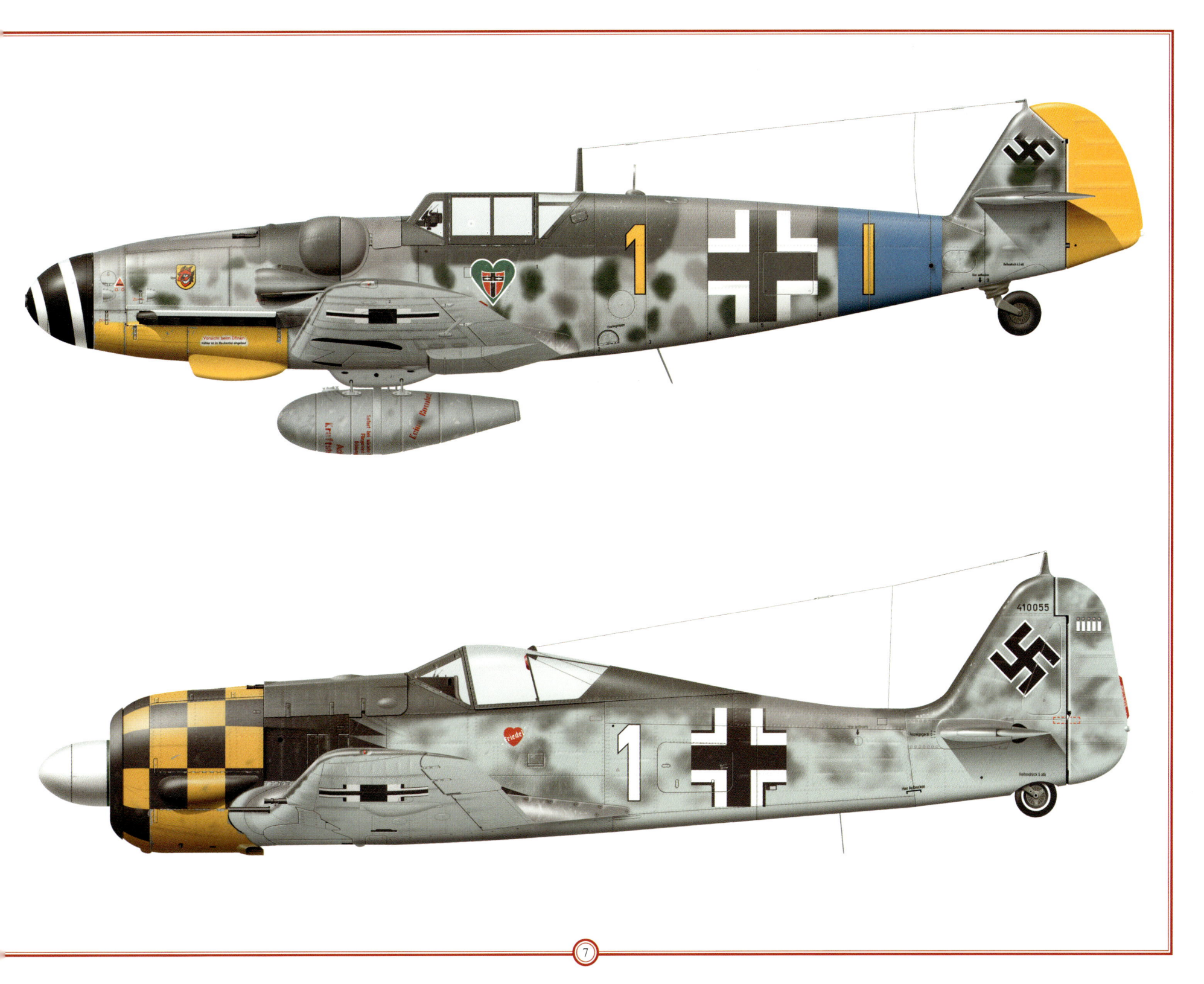

North American P-51D-15-NA
"GLAMOROUS GLEN III" s/n: 44-14888 • Capt. "Chuck" Yeager • 357th FG

Notes:
Yeager's score stood at 11.5 kills when WWII ended.
The U.S. national insignia is the 'low visibility' type with Grey star and bars instead of White.
Charles Elwood Yeager was enshrined into the National Aviation Hall of Fame in 1973.

Colors:
Overall natural metal
Spinner: Yellow and Red striped • Prop Blades: Black with Yellow tips
Identification markings: Red and Yellow checks, Red rudder
Anti-glare panel: Olive Drab

References:
Airfoil #5 by Steve Sheflin, 1987.

Messerschmitt Bf 109 G-14
W. Nr.: 464549 • II./JG 52 • Neubiberg, Germany • 1945

Colors:
Undersurfaces: RLM 76
Uppersurfaces: RLM 74, RLM 75
Upperwing and horizontal stabilizer: RLM 74, RLM 75
Spinner: Black with White Spiral • Prop Blades: RLM 70

References:
Original photos from the collection of James V. Crow

GLAMOROUS GLEN III
Capt. Yeager
B6
Y
414888

464549
C3
21
Vorsicht beim Öffnen

Messerschmitt Me 262 A-1a

III./KG(J) 54 • 1945

Colors:
Undersurfaces: RLM 76
Uppersurfaces: RLM 83
Upperwing and horizontal stabilizer: RLM 83
RV Bands: RLM 24 and White checks

References:
Original photos from the collection of Jim Crow
Experten #2a "Checkmate" by D. Brown & D. Wadman. Experten Publications, 1997.
Jäger Blatt Magazine, 1/1996 issue. Article by Jan Horn on KG(J) units.

Messerschmitt Bf 109 G-5

Uffz. Gerhard Kroll • 9./JG 54 • 1944

Colors:
Undersurfaces: RLM 76
Uppersurfaces: RLM 74, RLM 75 with RLM 76 overspray
Spinner: Yellow • Prop Blades: RLM 70

References:
Messerschmitt Bf 109 F, G, & K Series by J. Prien & P. Rodeike. Schiffer, 1993.
Original photo from the collection of Jerry Crandall
Interview with Kroll by Jerry Crandall

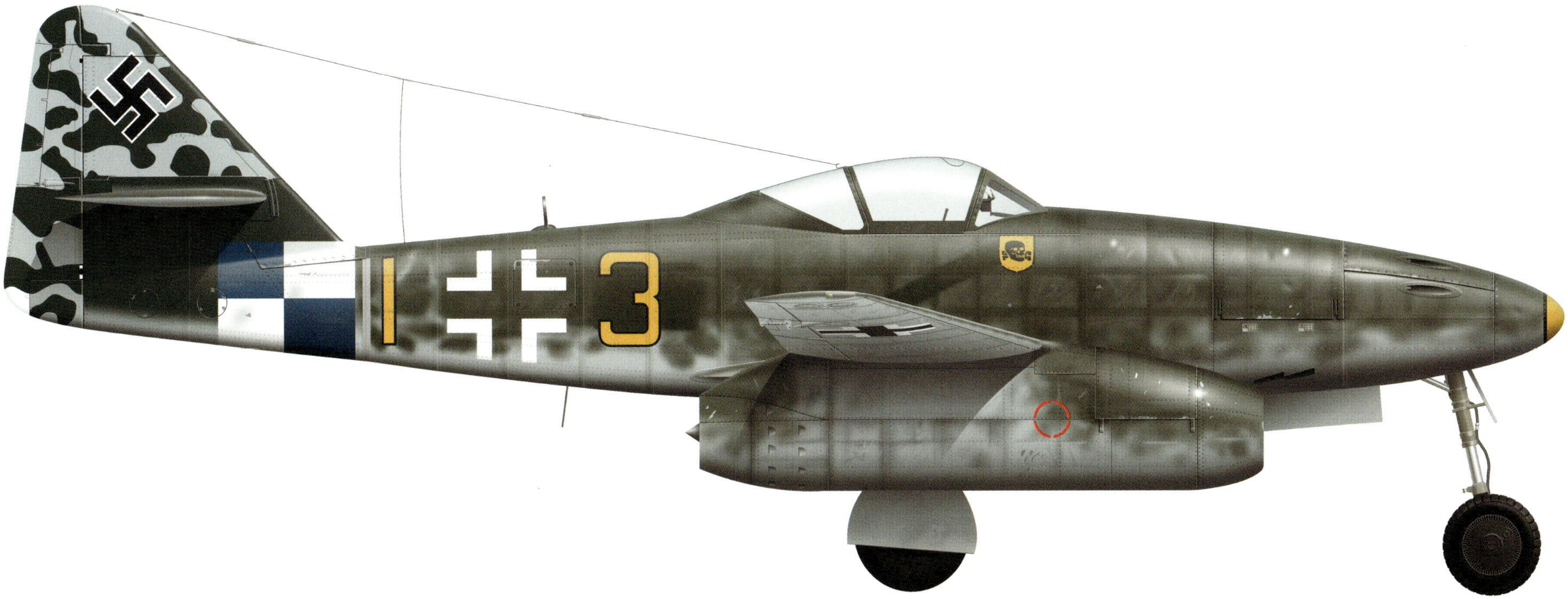

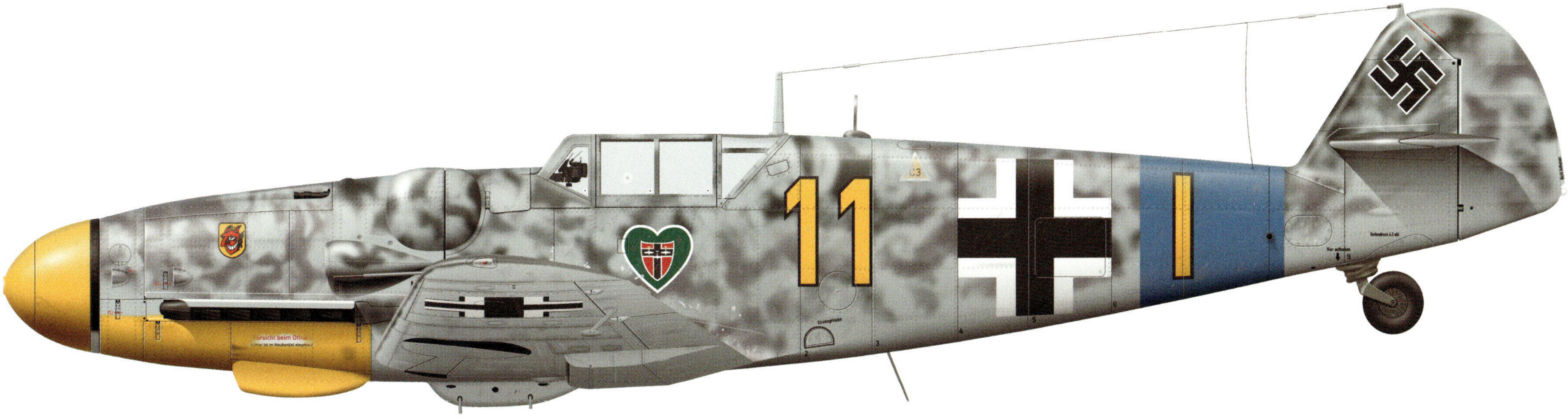

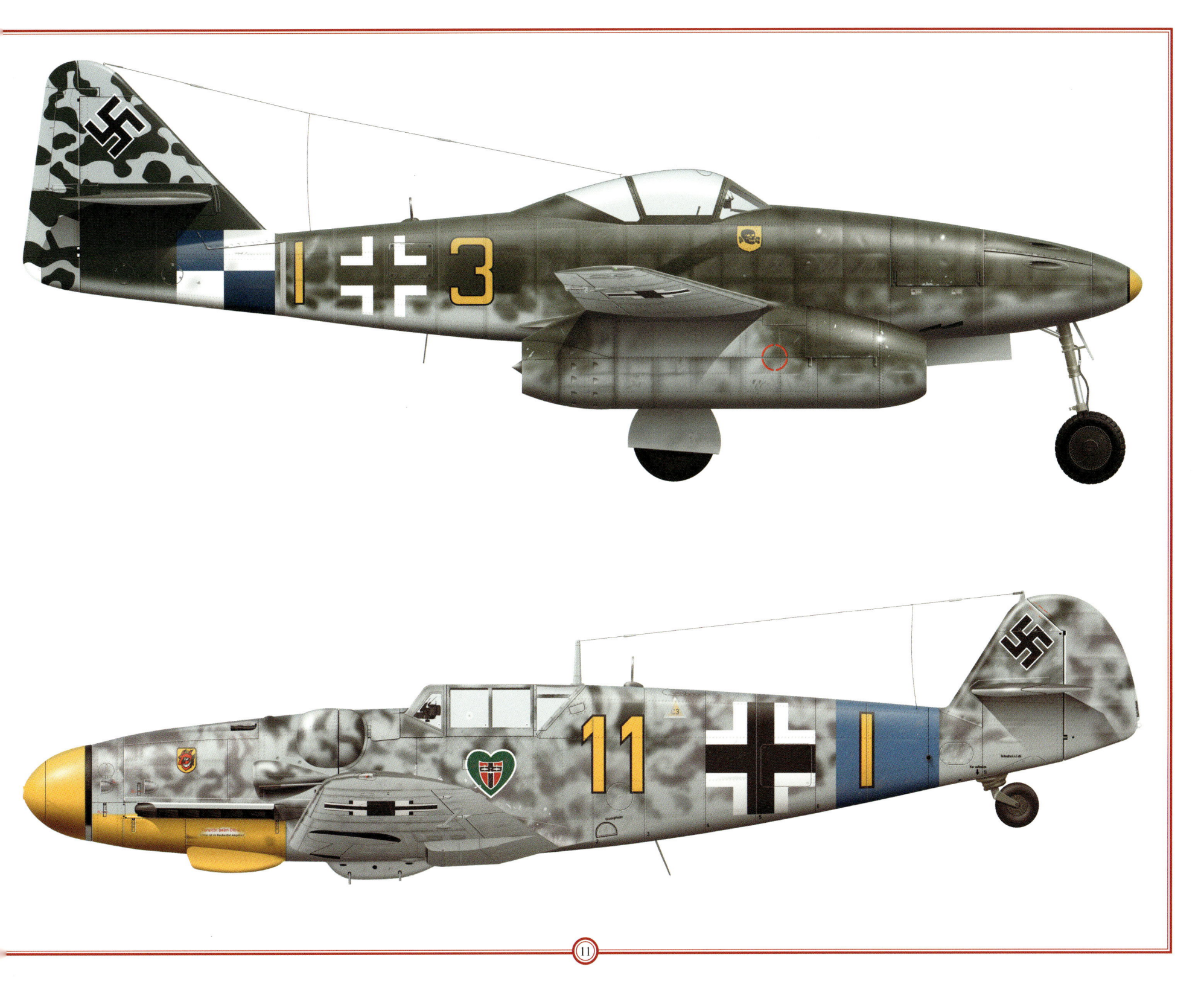

Focke-Wulf Fw 190 A-7/R2

W. Nr.: 643701 • 2./JG 11 • Rotenburg, Germany • March 1944

Notes:
Fuselage national markings are heavily oversprayed for reduced visibility

Colors:
Undersurfaces: RLM 76
Uppersurfaces: RLM 74, RLM 75
Upperwing and horizontal stabilizer: RLM 74, RLM 75
Spinner: Black with White Spiral • Propeller Blades: RLM 70

References:
Focke Wulf Jagdflugzeug Fw190A, Dora & Ta152 by Peter Rodeike.

Curtiss Hawk H81A-2 (P-40B)

Charlie Bond • 1st Pursuit Squadron, American Volunteer Group (A.V.G.) • China • 1941

Notes:
The upper surface pattern was applied using rubber templates resulting in a fairly hard edged camouflage similar to RAF fighters. While the author could not find any photos showing the kill markings on the fuselage side, Bond clearly remembers that nine full flags and one flag cut diagonally were applied to his aircraft.
For their group's courage, duty, innovation, and tenacity in the face of adversity, the AVG Flying Tigers were the recipients of the National Aviation Hall of Fame's 1999 "Milton Caniff Spirit of Flight Award."

Colors:
Undersurfaces: Sky
Uppersurfaces: Dark Earth, Dark Green
Prop blades: Black with Yellow tips

References:
Original photos & interviews with Bond

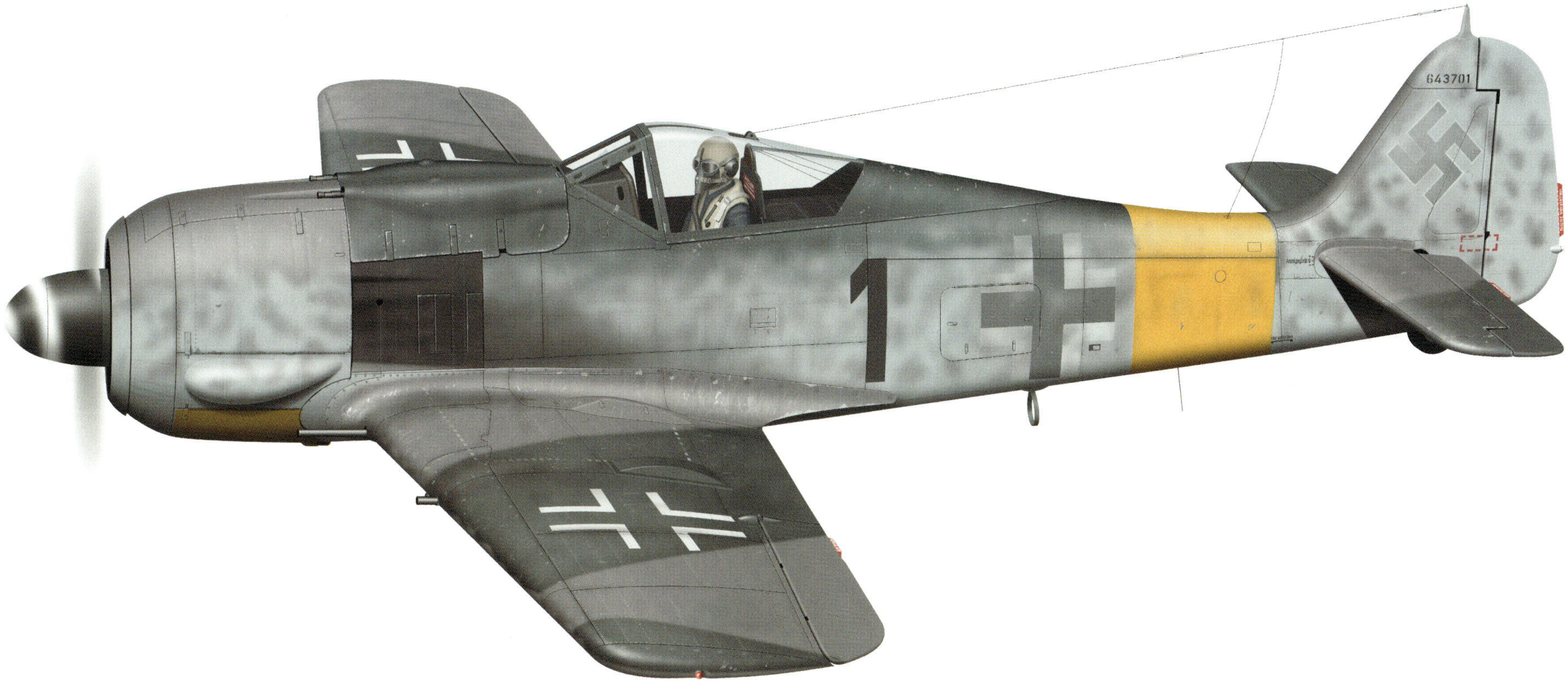

643701
1

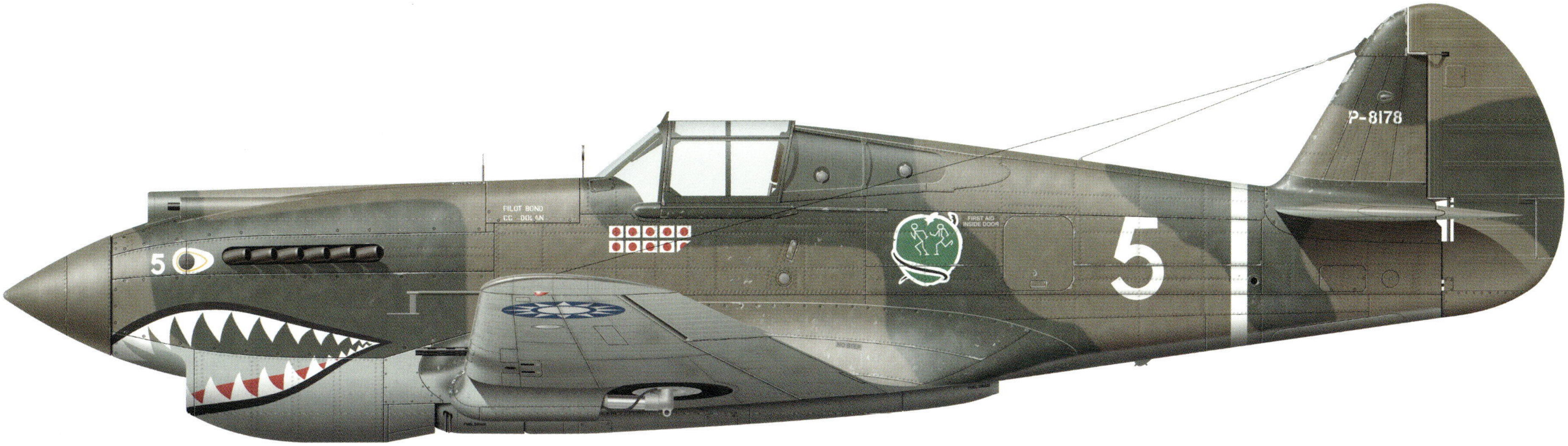

P-8178
PILOT BOND
CC DOLAN
FIRST AID
INSIDE DOOR
5
5

Vought F4U-1A

Jim Streig • VF-17 • March 1944

Notes:
Pilot credited with 5 kills, six appear in photo

Colors:
Standard U.S. Navy tri-color scheme consisting of Non Specular Sea Blue, Intermediate Blue and Non Specular White
Prop Blades: Black with Yellow tips

References:
Markings of the Aces, US NAVY Book 2 by Charles Graham & Richard Hill. Kookaburra Technical Pub., 1972.

Messerschmitt Me 262 A-1a

Rudi Sinner • Stab. III./JG 7

Notes:
Wgr. 21cm rockets and racks installed under the fuselage.
The swastika and tail camouflage are provisional as this area was not visible in the reference photo.

Colors:
Undersurfaces: RLM 76 • Uppersurfaces: RLM 82 & RLM 70

References:
Messerschmitt Me 262-Development, Testing, Production by W. Radinger & W. Schick. Schiffer, 1993.

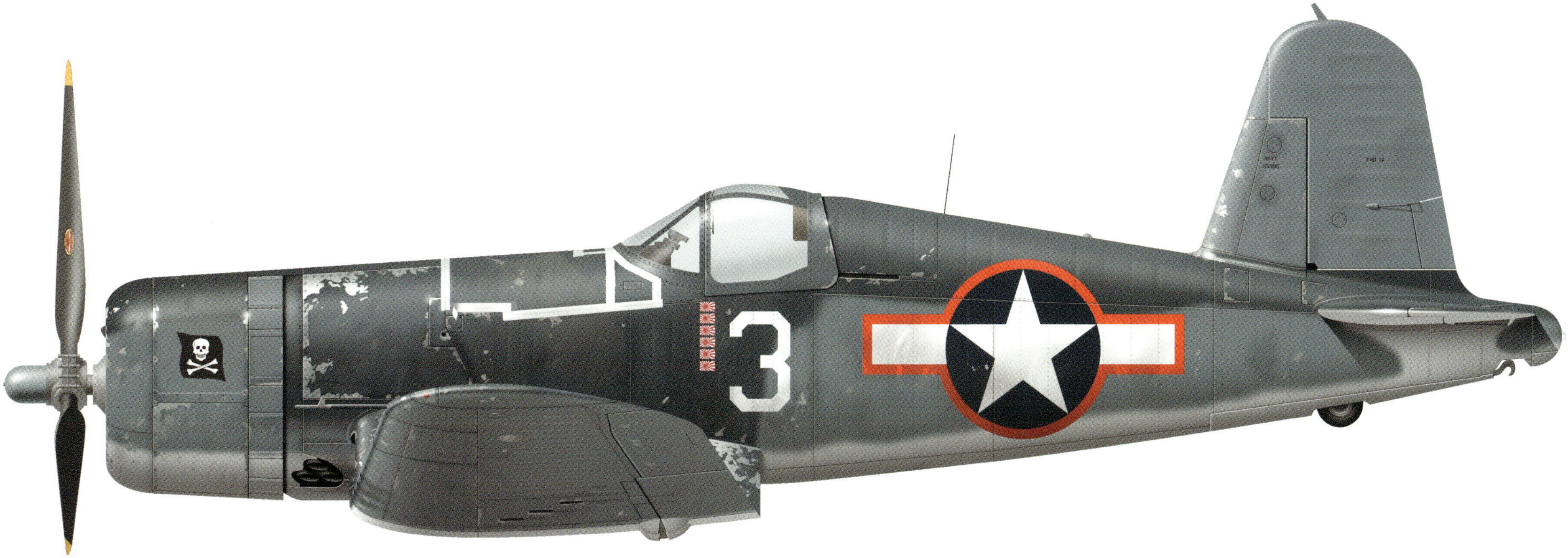

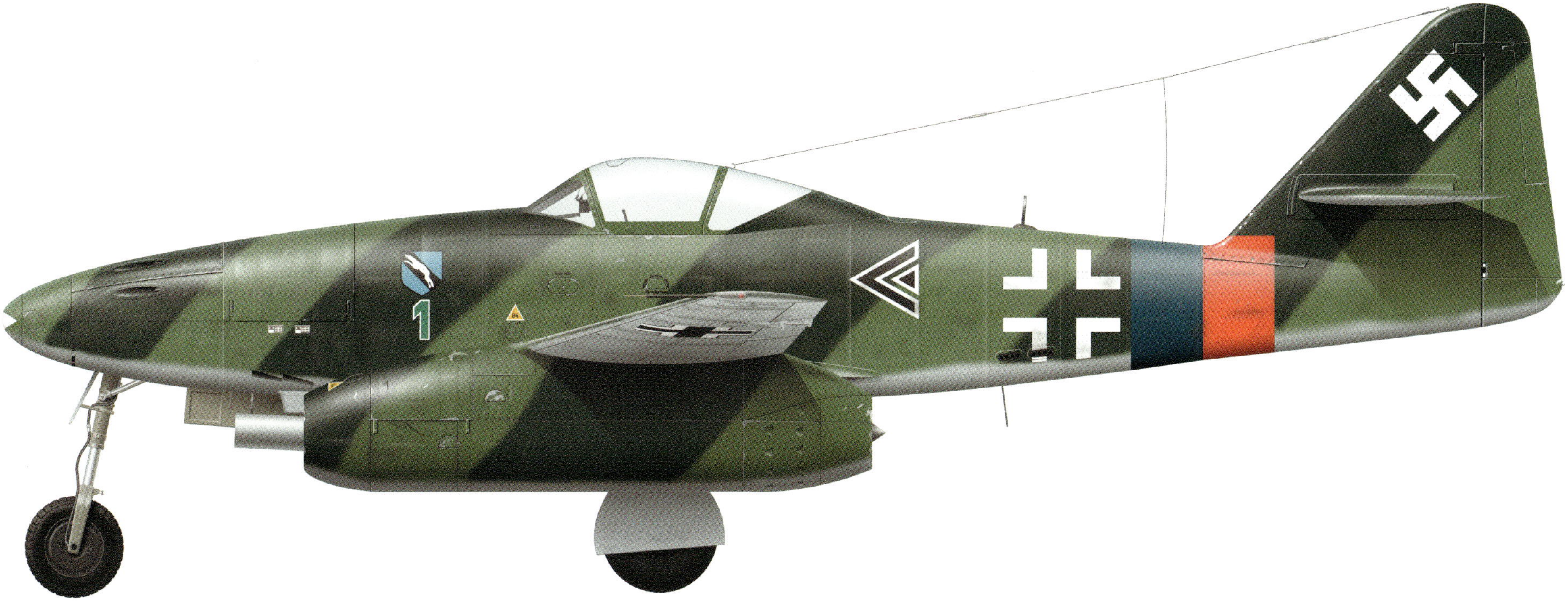

Supermarine Spitfire Mk Vb

Capt. Jan Zumbach No 303 Kosciuszko Squadron RAF 1942

Notes:
Zumbach flew several Spitfire Mk Vb fighters that had the code RF•D and the Duck artwork forward of the canopy.
Some confusion might arise if a photo of a different RF•D were compared to this profile.

Colors:
Undersurfaces: Medium Sea Grey • Uppersurfaces: Ocean Grey, Dark Green
Spinner: Sky with Red tip • Prop blades: Black with Yellow tips

References:
Polish Air Forces 1939-1945, Squadron Signal Pub. by Jan Koniarek.
Pictorial History of Military Aircraft Edited by John Pimlott.

Focke-Wulf Fw 190 F-8/R1

1945

Notes:
ETC 71 racks installed under wings.
Yellow rudder and cowl stripe applied for air-to-ground recognition.

Colors:
Undersurfaces: RLM 76 • Uppersurfaces: RLM 82, RLM 75
Upperwing and horizontal stabilizer: RLM 82, RLM 75
Spinner: Black with White Spiral • Prop Blades: RLM 70

References:
Monografie Lotnicze #17 Fw 190A/F/G by Adam Skupiewski. AJ Press, 1994.
Original photos

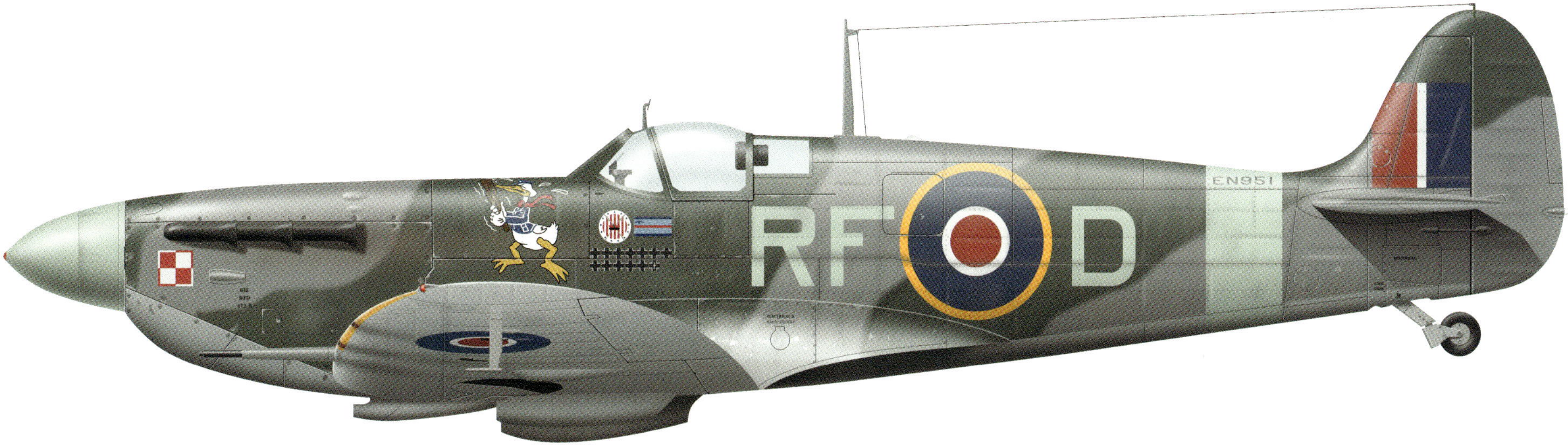
EN951
RF D
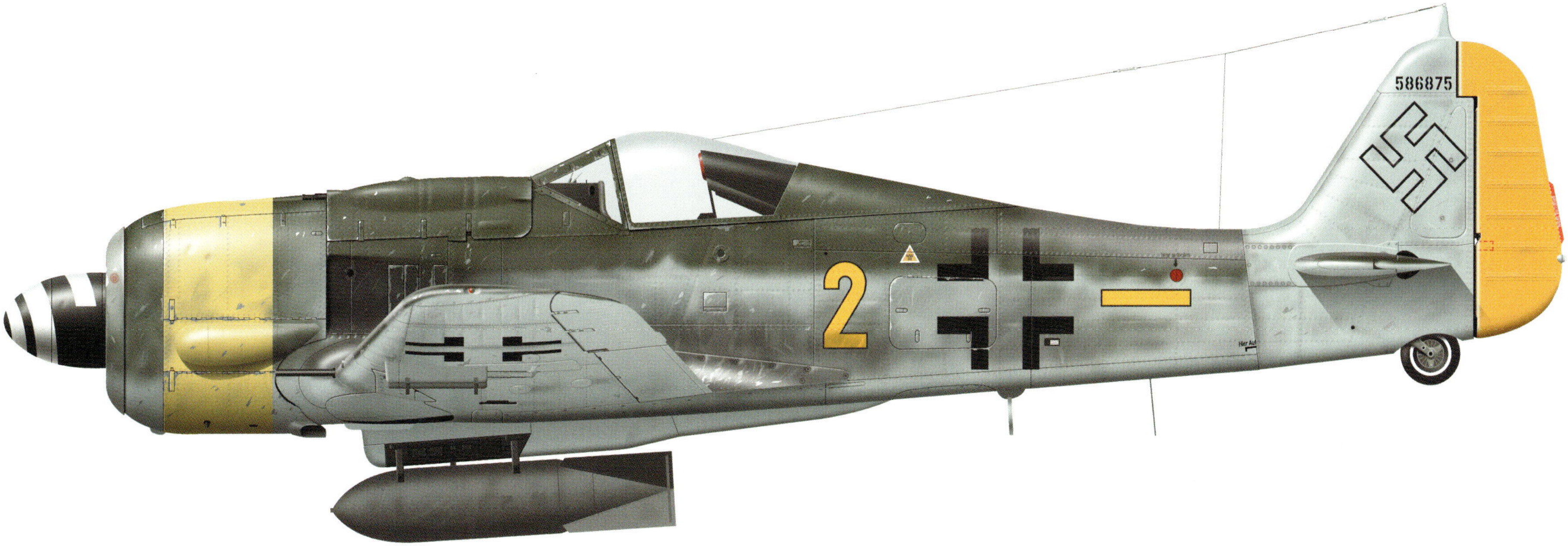
586875
2

North American P-51D-20-NA

"The Flying Undertaker" s/n: 44-72505 • Maj. William Shomo • 82nd TRS

Colors:
Overall natural metal
Spinner: Yellow • Prop Blades: Black with Yellow tips
Identification markings: Black with Yellow edge stripes
Anti-glare panel: Olive Drab

References:
Original photos

Messerschmitt Me 163 B-1a

W.Nr.:191454 • 6./JG 400 • 1945

Notes:
Vertical stabilizer has hand brushed paint along fin cap juncture. This has been interpreted as being
a rust colored primer (very common at this time) but could also have been RLM 74.

Colors:
Undersurfaces: RLM 76
Uppersurfaces: RLM 74, RLM 75
Forward fuselage and generator spinner: Yellow with Black trim
Landing skid: RLM 02

References:
War Prizes by Phil Butler. Midland Counties Publications, 1994.
Research assistance provided by Ken Merrick

19

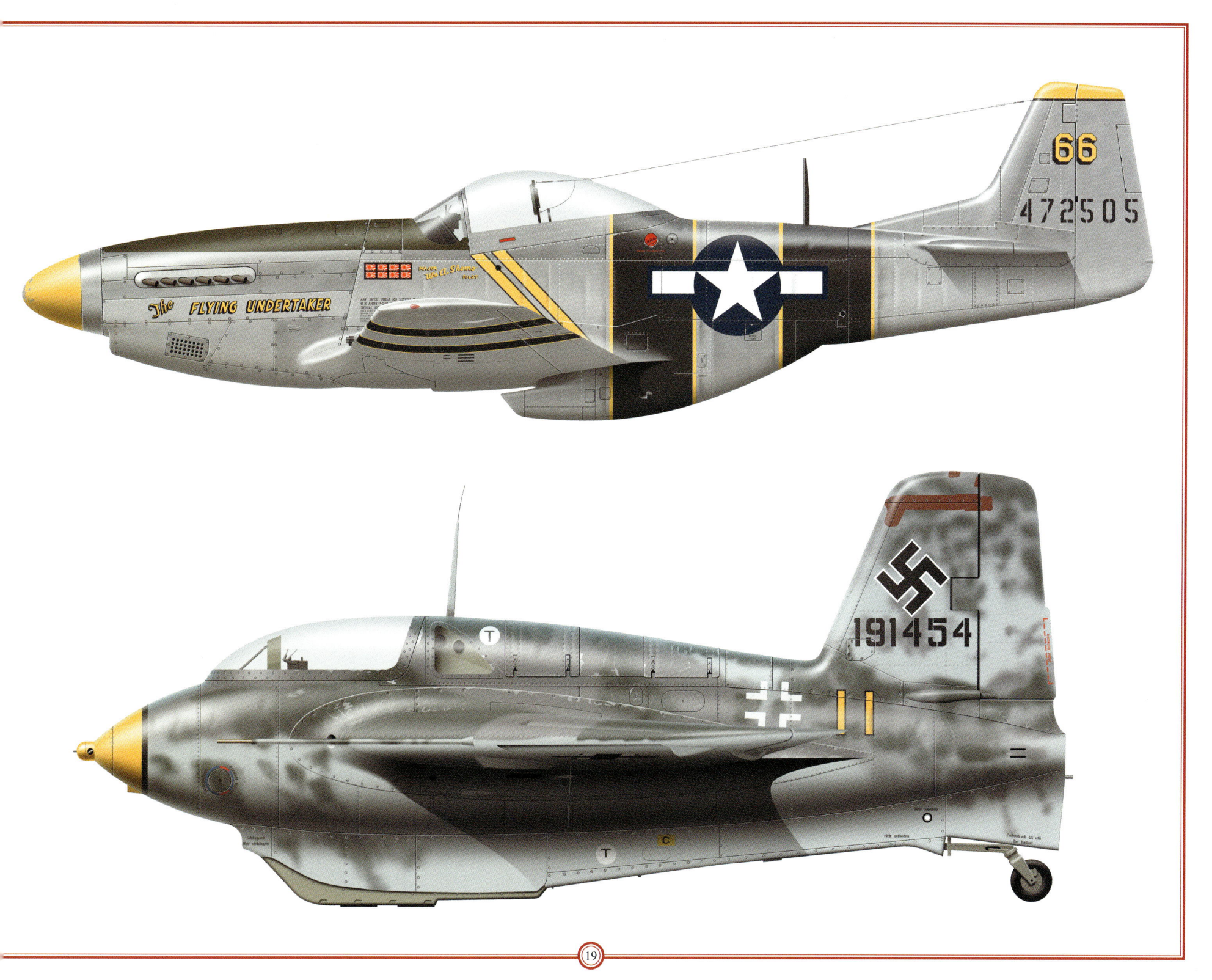

Messerschmitt Bf 109 E-3

W. Nr.: 7851? • Flown by Geschwaderadjudant • Stab. III./JG 27 • Feb. 1941

Colors:
Undersurfaces: RLM 65
Uppersurfaces: RLM 71, RLM 02
Spinner: RLM 70 • Prop Blades: RLM 70

References:
Aircraft of the Luftwaffe Fighter Aces I by Bernd Barbas. Schiffer Publishing Ltd., 1995.

Vought F4U-1A

Lt. Stout • VMF-422.

Colors:
Standard U.S. Navy tri-color scheme consisting of Non Specular Sea Blue, Intermediate Blue and Non Specular White
Prop Blades: Black with Yellow tips

References:
F4U Corsair in action by Jim Sullivan. Squadron Signal Publications, 1994.

21

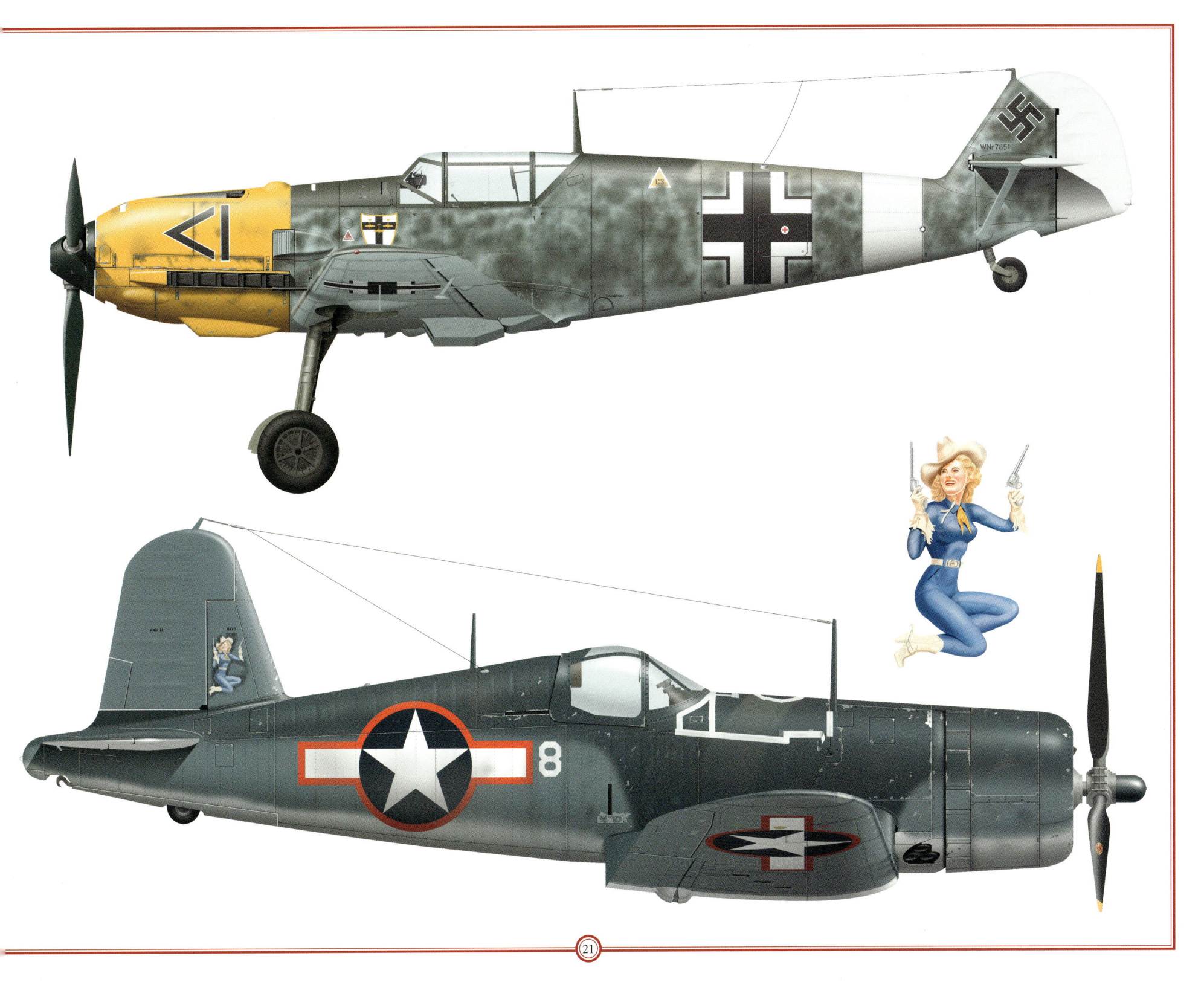

North American P-51D-20-NA

s/n: 44-72199 • Capt. Charles E. Weaver • 362nd FS, 357th FG

Notes:
8 air and 3 ground kills

Colors:
Overall natural metal
Spinner: Yellow and Red • Prop Blades: Black with Yellow tips
Identification markings: Yellow and Red checker pattern on forward fuselage
Anti-glare panel: Olive Drab

References:
Airfoil #5 by Steve Sheflin, Airfoil Publications, 1987.
Flying Scoreboards by E. McDowell, Squadron Signal Publications, 1993.
Aces of the Eighth by G. Stafford, Squadron Signal Publications, 1973.
P-51 Mustang by Larry Davis, Squadron Signal Publications, 1995.
Fighters of the Mighty Eighth by William Hess, Motorbooks, 1990.

Vought F4U-1D

VF-5, CV-13 USS Franklin

Colors:
Standard U.S. Navy Glossy Sea Blue scheme
Prop Blades: Black with Yellow tips

References:
Original Photo

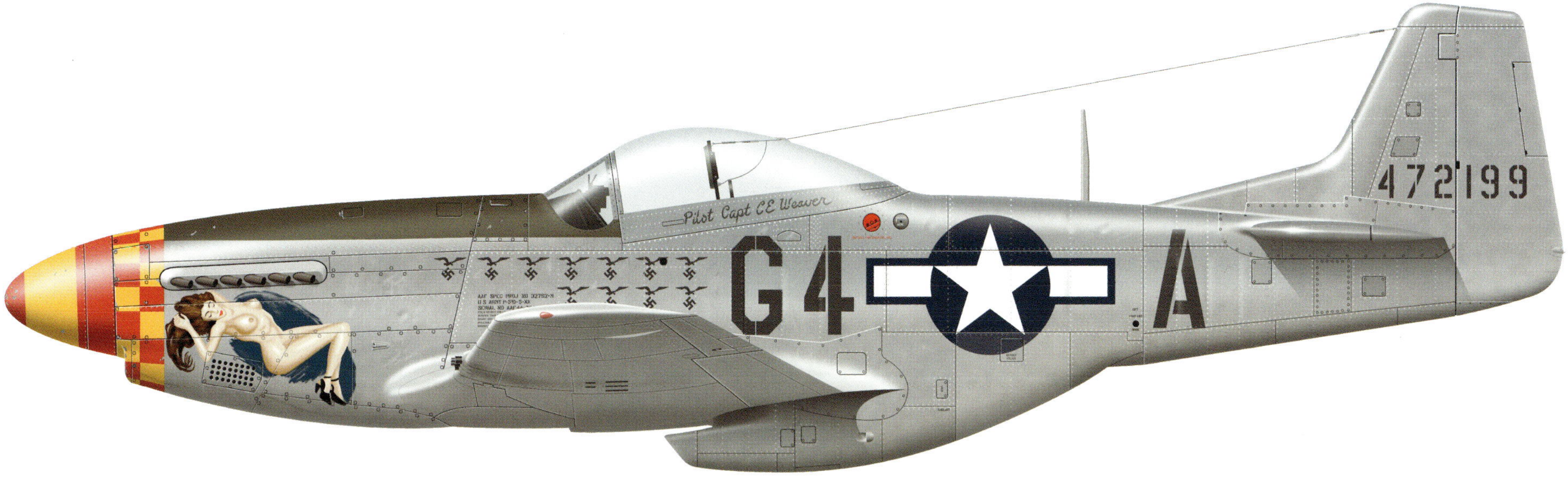
472199
Pilot Capt CE Weaver
G4
A

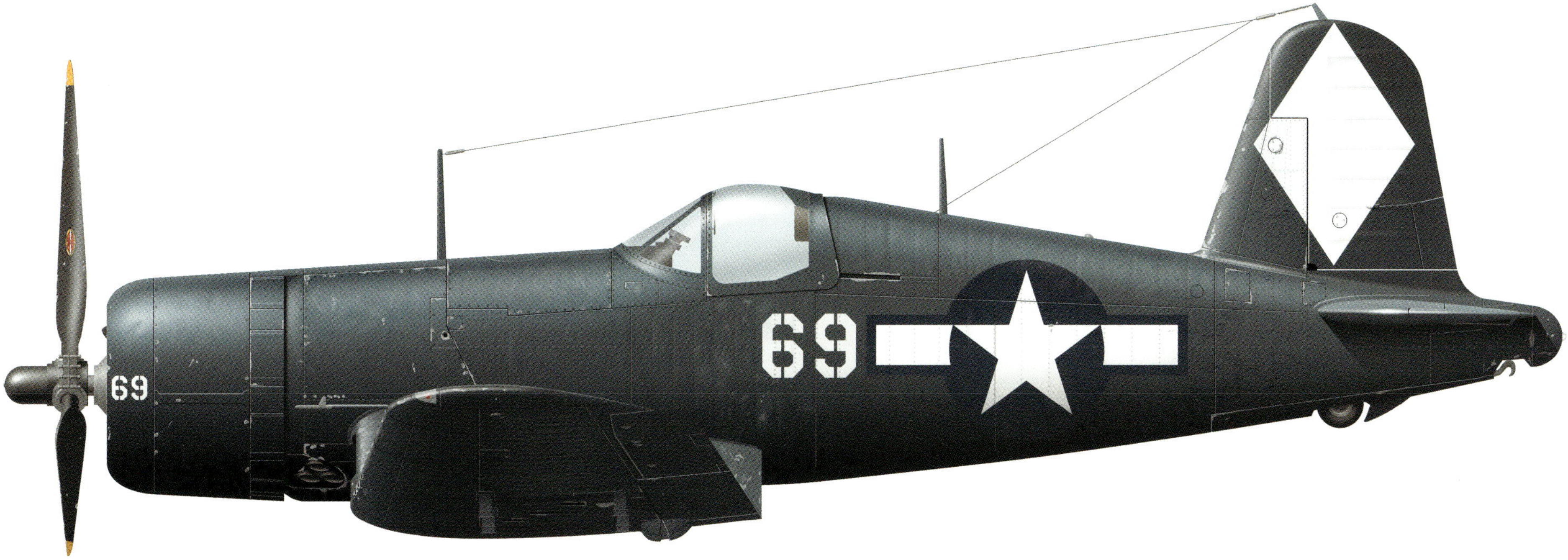
69
69

Messerschmitt Bf 109 G-10(?)

Stab 1./KG(J) 6

Notes:
Only mid fuselage is visible in photo (from cockpit to aft edge of RV band)-the cowl and tail markings/camouflage are provisional.

Colors:
Undersurfaces: RLM 76
Uppersurfaces: RLM 75 & RLM 83
Prop blades: RLM 70
Spinner: Black with white spiral

References:
Bf 109 G/H, Militaria #47

Focke-Wulf Fw 190 A-7

W. Nr.: 340283 • Fw. Gerhard Geise • 3./JG 1

Colors:
Undersurfaces: RLM 76
Uppersurfaces: RLM 74, RLM 75
Upperwing and horizontal stabilizer: RLM 74, RLM 75
Spinner: RLM 04 • Propeller Blades: RLM 70

References:
JG 1 Historie de la Jagdgeschwader 1 "Oesau" by Eric Mombeek. Collection HISTOIRE DE L'AVIATION No 3, 1997.

25

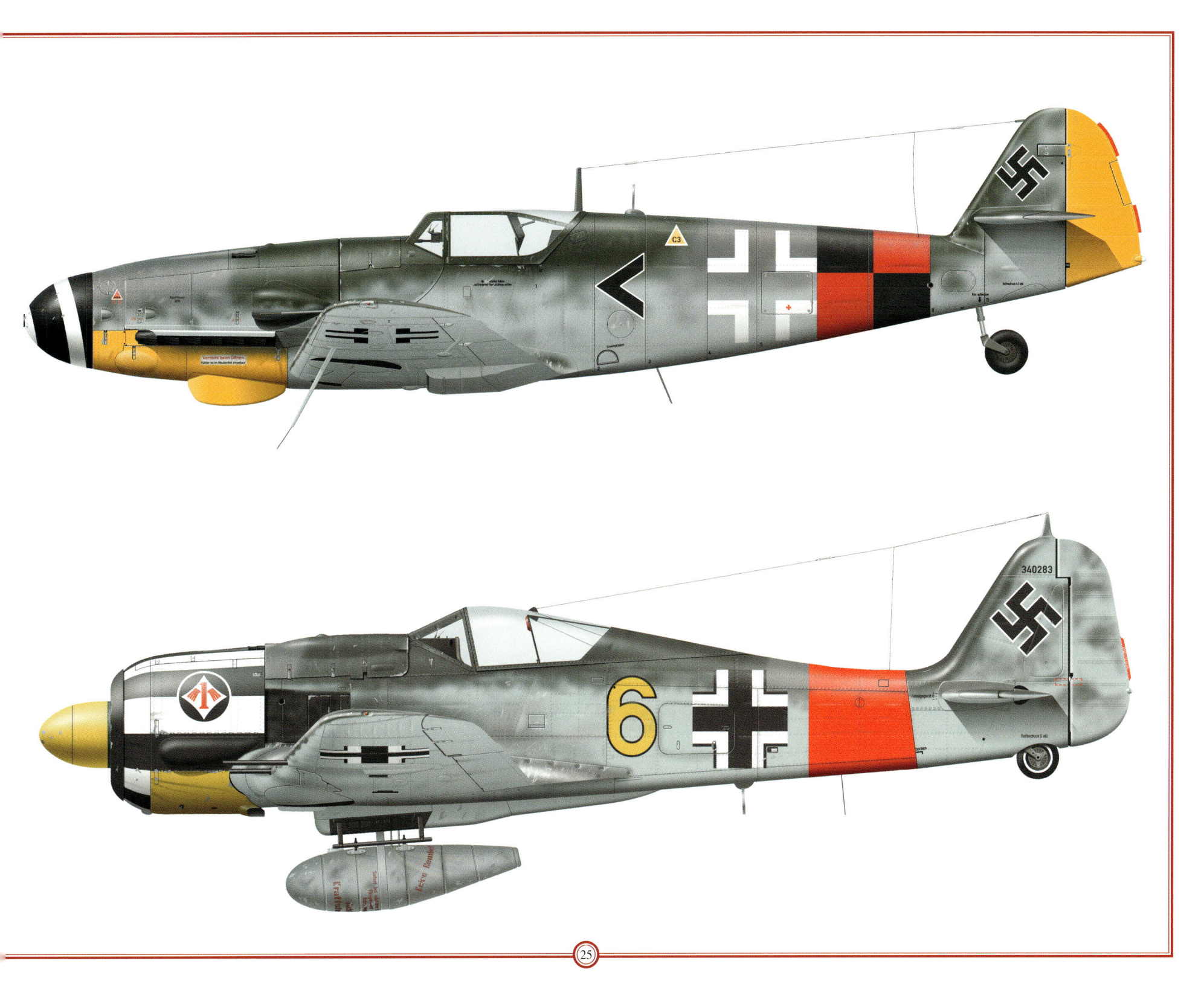

North American P-51D-20-NA

s/n: 44-63607 • Lt. Col Glenn T Eagleston (CO 353 FS) • 353 FS, 354th FG

Notes:
18.5 official kills, a/c marked with 23.5

Colors:
Overall natural metal
Spinner: Yellow • Prop Blades: Black with Yellow tips
Anti-glare panel: Olive Drab

References:
Original photos
P-51 Mustang by Larry Davis, Squadron Signal Publications, 1995.
Fighters of the Mighty Eighth by William Hess, Motorbooks, 1990.

Curtiss Hawk H81A-2 (P-40B)

Fin # P-8127
Robert Layher & John Petach • 2nd Pursuit Squadron, American Volunteer Group (A.V.G.) • China • 1941

Notes:
The upper surface pattern was applied using rubber templates resulting in a fairly hard edged camouflage similar to RAF fighters.
This aircraft was later transferred to the 3rd Pursuit Squadron where the fuselage band was repainted Red and a Hell's Angel insignia was applied on the port side.
For their group's courage, duty, innovation, and tenacity in the face of adversity, the AVG Flying Tigers were the recipients of the
National Aviation Hall of Fame's 1999 "Milton Caniff Spirit of Flight Award."

Colors:
Undersurfaces: Sky
Uppersurfaces: Dark Earth, Dark Green
Prop blades: Black with Yellow tips

References:
Original photos & interviews with Layher

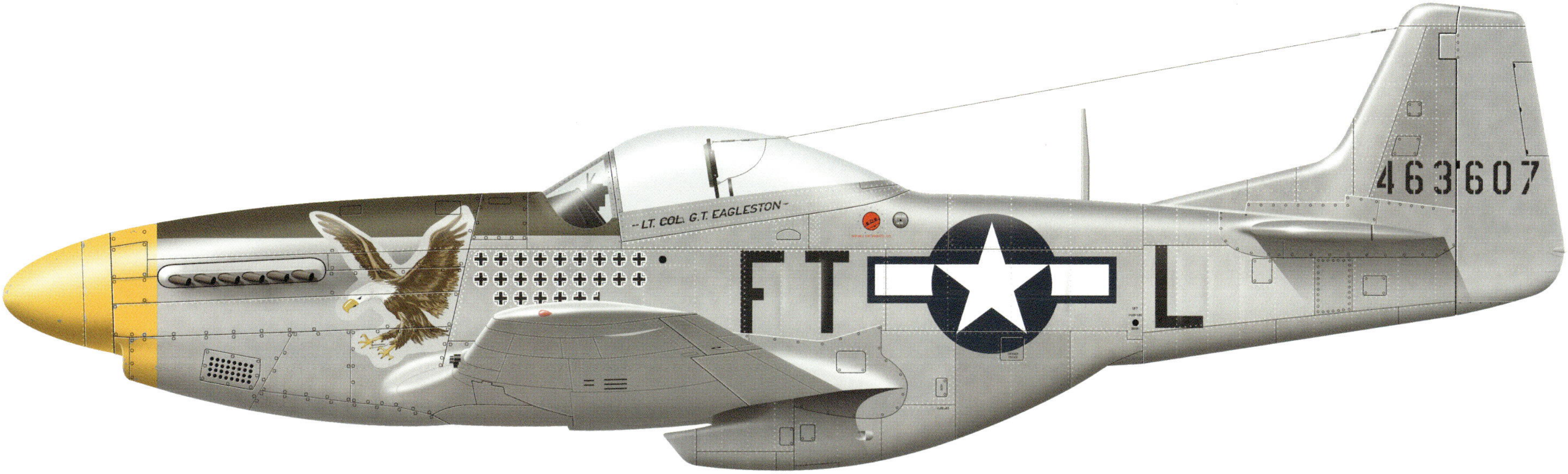
LT. COL. G.T. EAGLESTON
FT L
463607

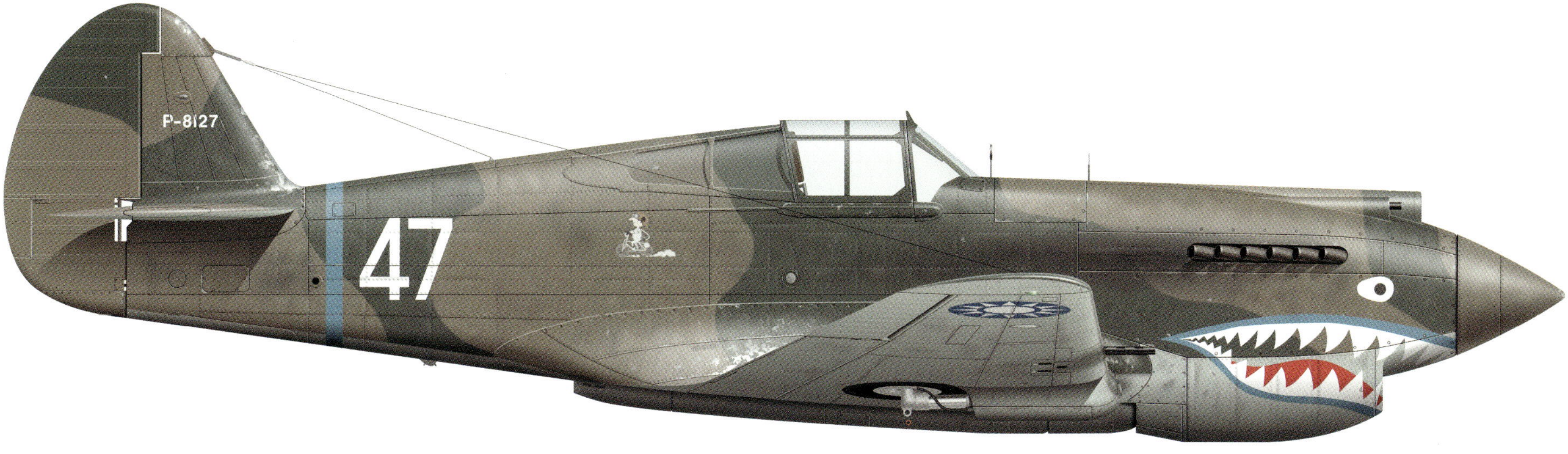
P-8127
47

Focke-Wulf Fw 190 D-9

W. Nr.: 210003 • Oblt. Hans Dortenmann • 12./JG 54

Notes:
This illustration is based on pilot's description and photos of aircraft *after* it had been repainted in new color scheme

Colors:
Undersurfaces: RLM 76
Uppersurfaces: RLM 75, RLM 83
Spinner: Black with White Spiral
Prop Blades: RLM 70

References:
Green Hearts, First in Combat with the Dora 9 by Axel Urbanke. Eagle Editions Ltd., 1998.

Grumman F4F-4

Capt. Joe Foss • VMF-121 • Guadalcanal • November 12, 1942

Notes:
This profile is provisional based on information provided by Foss and research by Barrett Tillman.
White 50 was the Wildcat in which Foss made his 20th, 21st and 22nd kills (a Zero and two 'Bettys') on November 12, 1942.
Foss ended the war with 26 confirmed victories, and was later elected Governor of South Dakota.
Joseph Jacob Foss was enshrined into the National Aviation Hall of Fame in 1984.

Colors:
Standard U.S. Navy two tone scheme consisting of Blue Gray over Light Gray
Prop Blades: Black with Yellow tips

References:
Interview with Joe Foss
Research assistance provided by Barrett Tillman

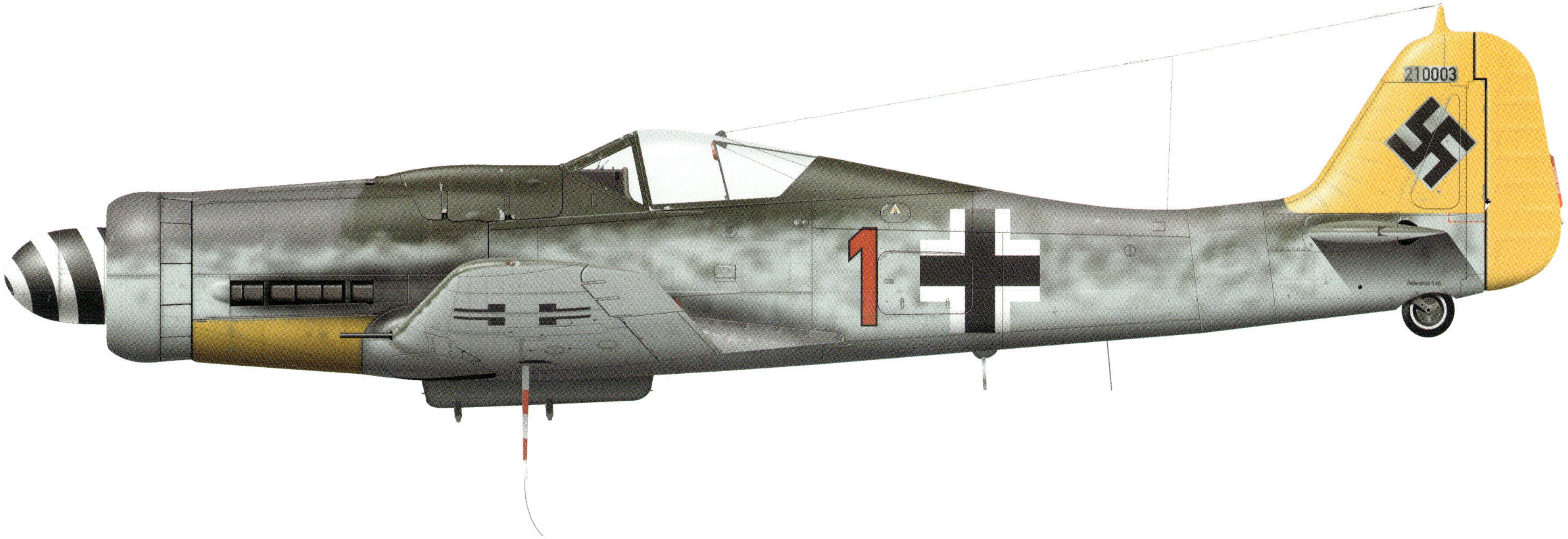
210003
1

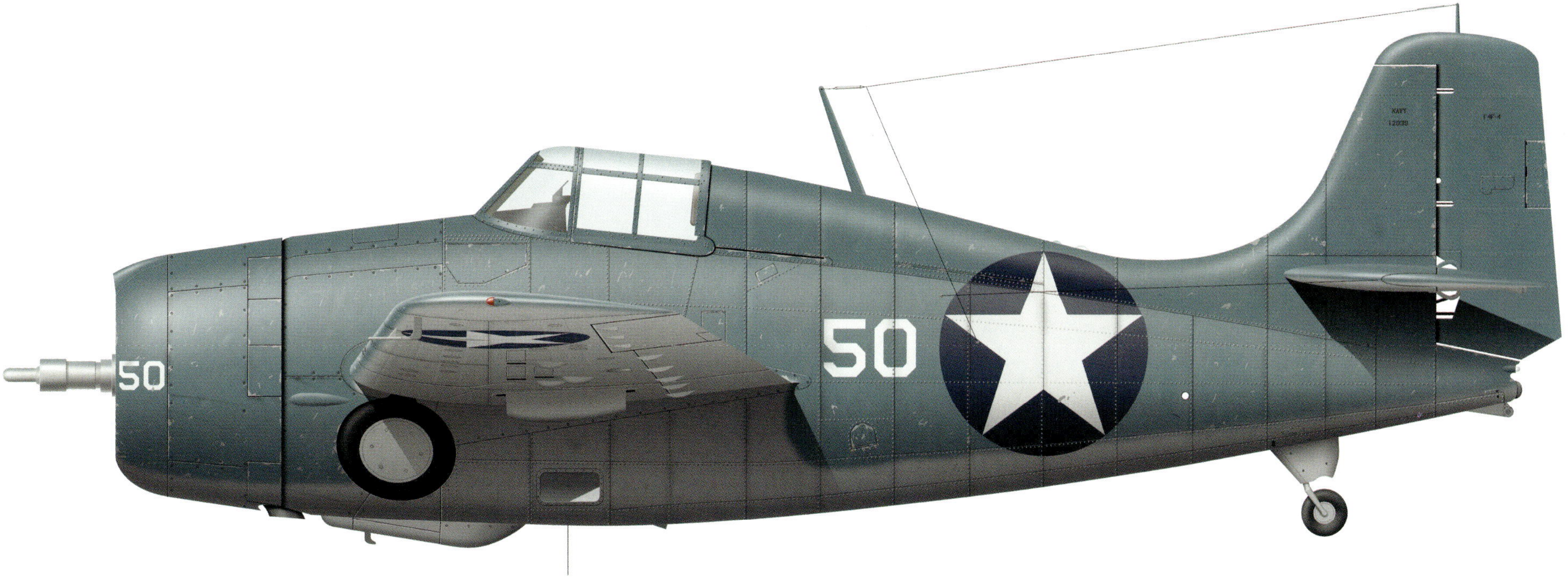
50
50

Curtiss Hawk H81A-2 (P-40B)

Fin # P-8109
Charles Older • 3rd Pursuit Squadron, American Volunteer Group (A.V.G.) • China • 1941

Notes:
The upper surface pattern was applied using rubber templates resulting in a fairly hard edged camouflage similar to RAF fighters.
Interior of shark mouth painted light blue (assumed to be same blue as Chinese insignia which faded rapidly once applied).
For their group's courage, duty, innovation, and tenacity in the face of adversity, the AVG Flying Tigers were the recipients of the
National Aviation Hall of Fame's 1999 "Milton Caniff Spirit of Flight Award."

Colors:
Undersurfaces: Sky
Uppersurfaces: Dark Earth, Dark Green
Prop blades: Black with Yellow tips

References:
Original photos & interviews with Older

Messerschmitt Bf 109 G-10

W.Nr.: 130297 • Fw. Horst Petzschler • 10./JG 51 • Bulltofa, Sweden • 4 May 1945

Notes:
Note previous tactical number has been painted out with gray. No trim tabs on rudder.

Colors:
Undersurfaces: RLM 76
Uppersurfaces: RLM 75, RLM 83
Spinner: Black with White Spiral • Prop Blades: RLM 70

References:
The Luftwaffe in Sweden by Bo Widfelt. Monogram Aviation Publications.
Interview with Petzschler by Jerry Crandall

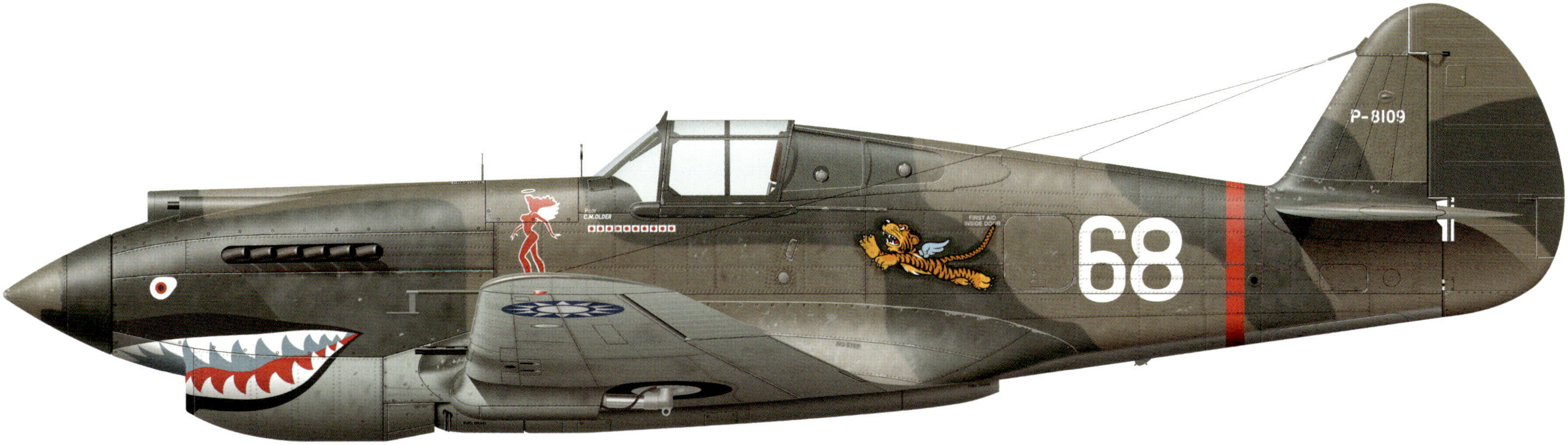
P-8109
68

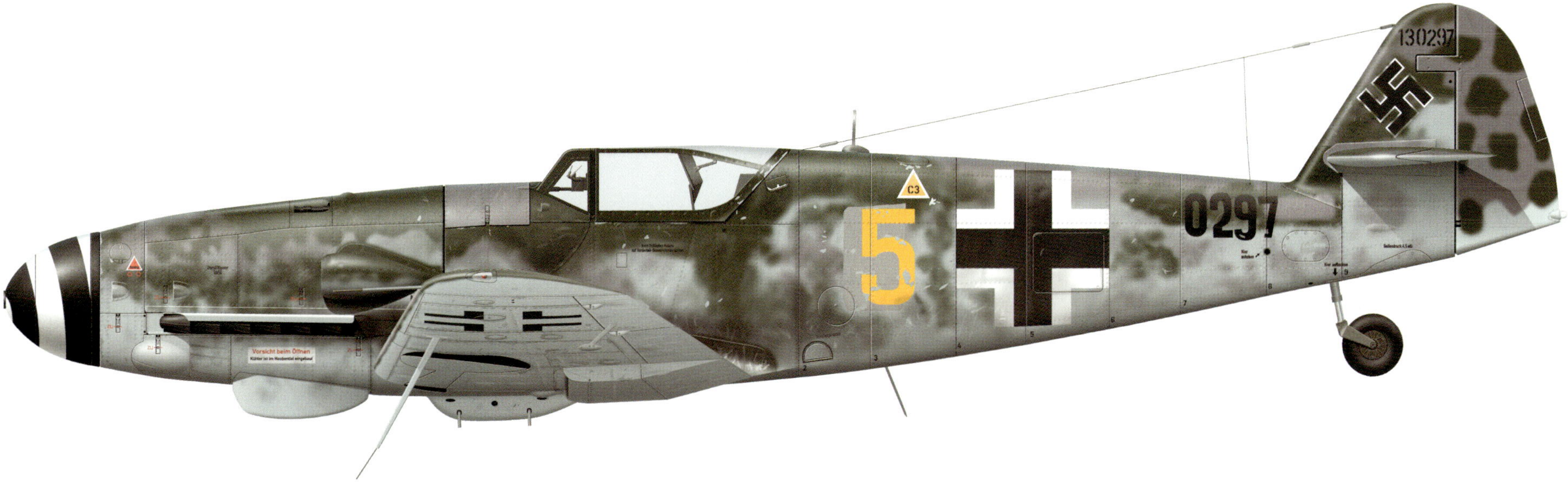
130297
C3
5
0297

Messerschmitt Bf 109 G-10

W.Nr.: 130xxx • I./JG 300

Notes:
This aircraft will undoubtably be the subject of much debate. Most researchers agree that this was a JG 300 aircraft, however some believe it may have belonged to JG 2. While most JG 300 Bf 109 G-10s had the type 110 cowl, several 130xxx series G-10s with type 100 cowls were flown by this unit. The badge on the cowl was blurred beyond recognition in the photo, so the selection of the 'wild boar' badge of JG 300 is pure speculation on my part.

Colors:
Undersurfaces: RLM 76
Uppersurfaces: RLM 75, RLM 83
Spinner: RLM 70 with 1/3 White • Prop Blades: RLM 70

References:
Broken Eagles #2 by Carl Hildebrandt. Fighter Pictorials, 1988.

Focke-Wulf Fw 190 D-9

Late war factory delivery scheme

Notes:
This illustration is an example of how the Langenhagen factory delivered many of their Fw 190 D aircraft in late 1944. Only uppersurface areas received camouflage paint, and all fabric control surfaces were either RLM 76 or primer.

References:
Interview with Klaus Hecht, line mechanic at Langenhagen late 1944. Interview conducted by Mr. John Quint.

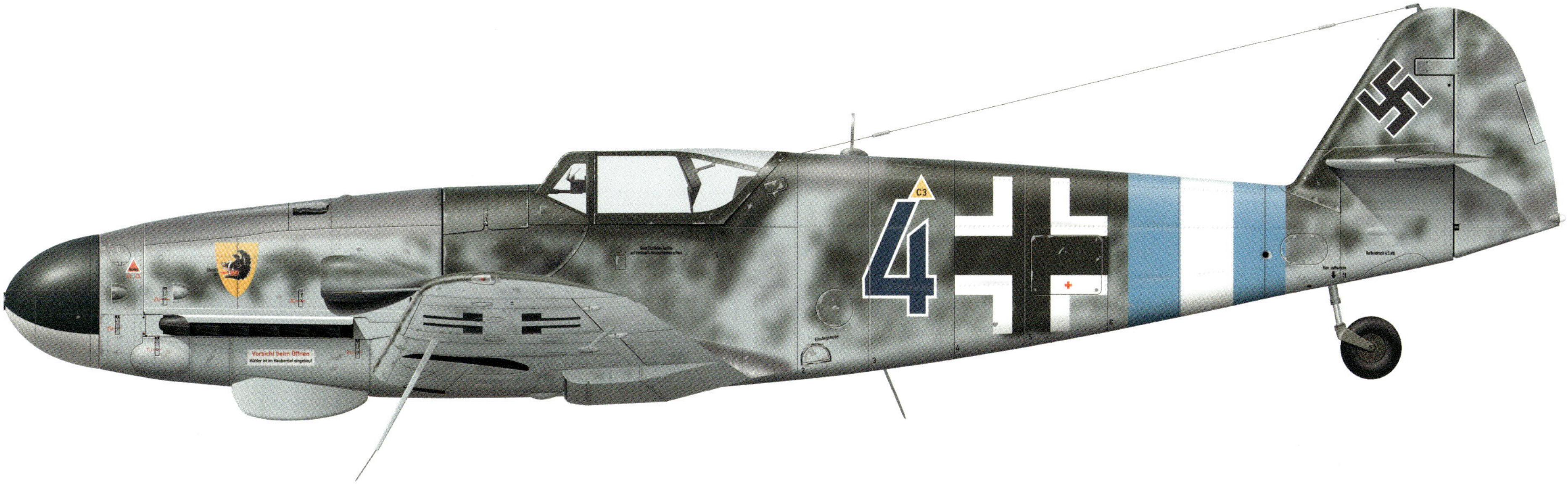
4
C3
Vorsicht beim Öffnen
Kühler ist im Haubenteil eingebaut

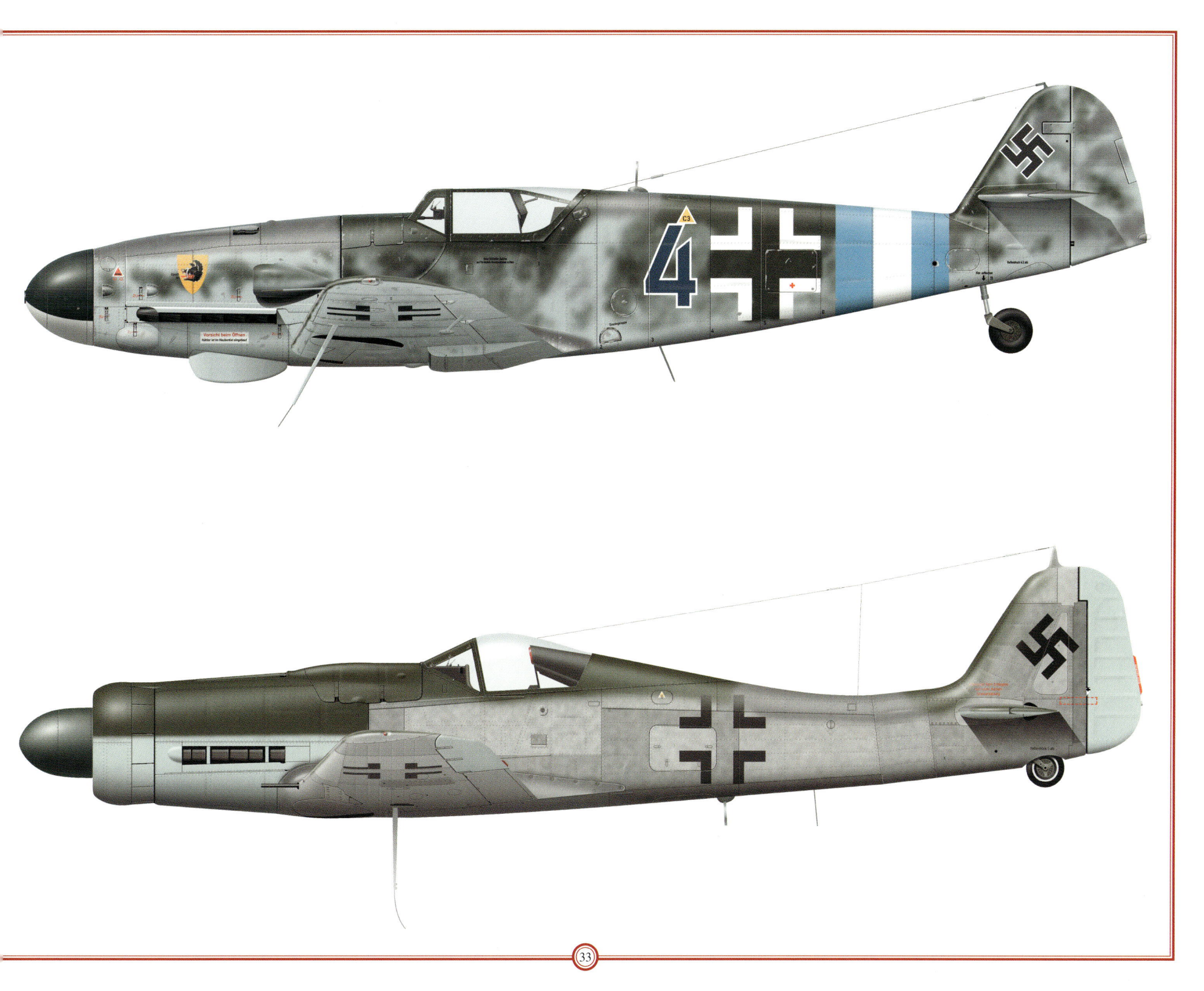

Focke-Wulf Fw 190 D-9

W.Nr.: 211018 • Stab JG 26

Notes:
RV bands have been oversprayed to aid in ground concealment.
Exhaust panel has stylized Black & White design that resembles those painted on early Fw 190 A's.

Colors:
Undersurfaces: RLM 76
Uppersurfaces: RLM 82, RLM 83
Spinner: Black with White Spiral
Prop Blades: RLM 70

References:
Green Hearts, First in Combat with the Dora 9 by Axel Urbanke. Eagle Editions Ltd., 1998.

Vought F4U-1D

VMF 312

Notes:
This F4U-1D has the old style braced canopy that was common to F4U-1A Corsairs.

Colors:
Standard U.S. Navy Glossy Sea Blue scheme
Prop Blades: Black with Yellow tips

References:
Original Photo

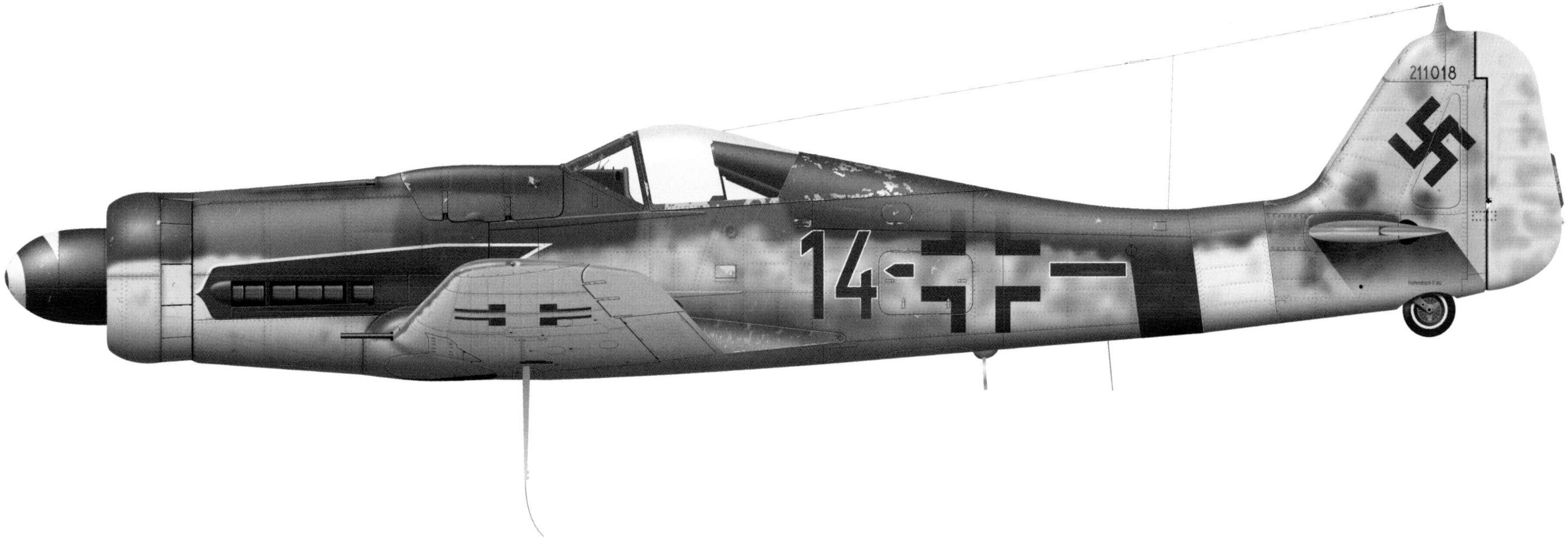
211018
14

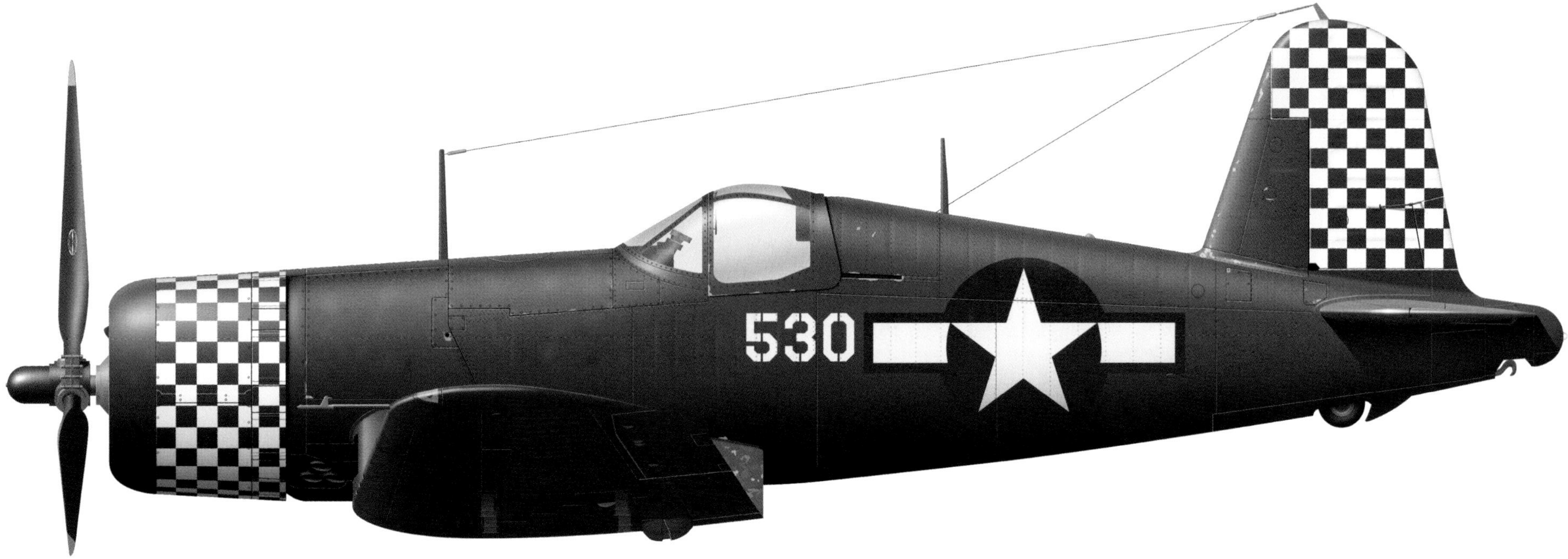
530

Focke-Wulf Fw 190 D-9

Uffz. Walter Stumpf • 7./JG 26 • Feb. 1945

Colors:
Undersurfaces: RLM 76
Uppersurfaces: RLM 82, RLM 83
Spinner: Black with White Spiral
Prop Blades: RLM 70

References:
Green Hearts, First in Combat with the Dora 9 by Axel Urbanke. Eagle Editions Ltd., 1998.

Messerschmitt Bf 109 G-6

Anton Hackl • Stab. III./JG 11 • Feb. 1944

Colors:
Undersurfaces: RLM 76 • Uppersurfaces: RLM 74, RLM 75
Spinner: 2/3 RLM 70, 1/3 White • Prop Blades: RLM 70

References:
Aircraft of the Luftwaffe Fighter Aces I by Bernd Barbas. Schiffer Publishing Ltd., 1995.

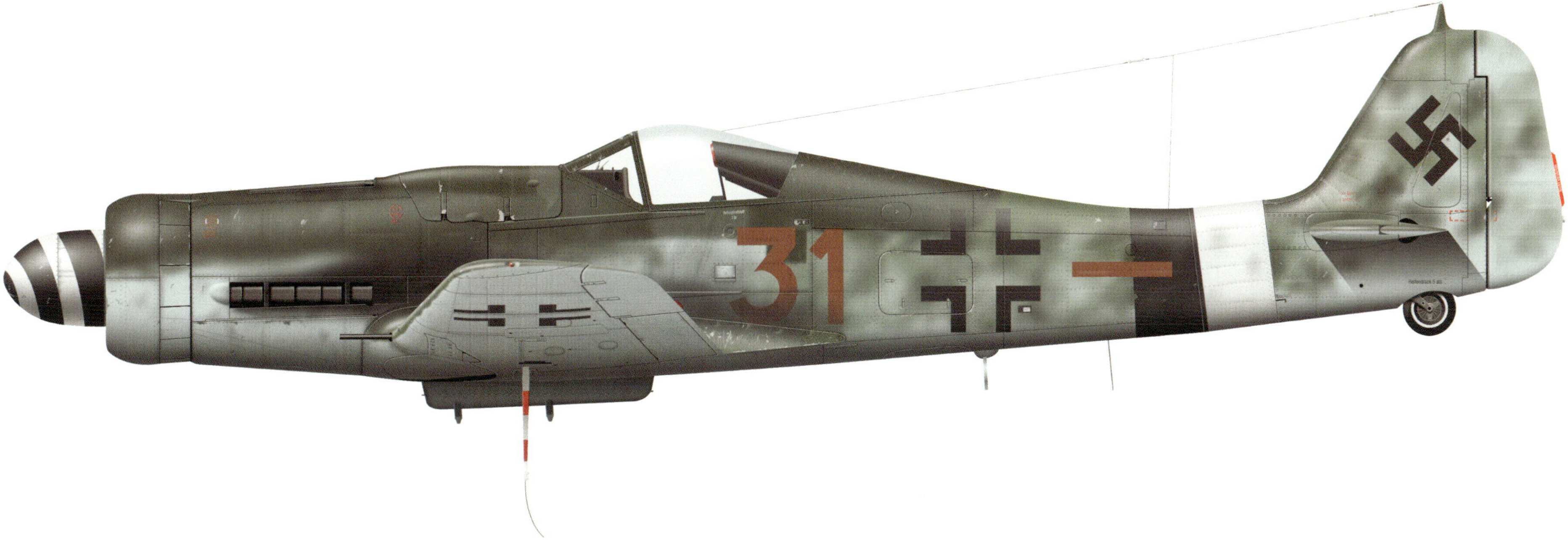
31

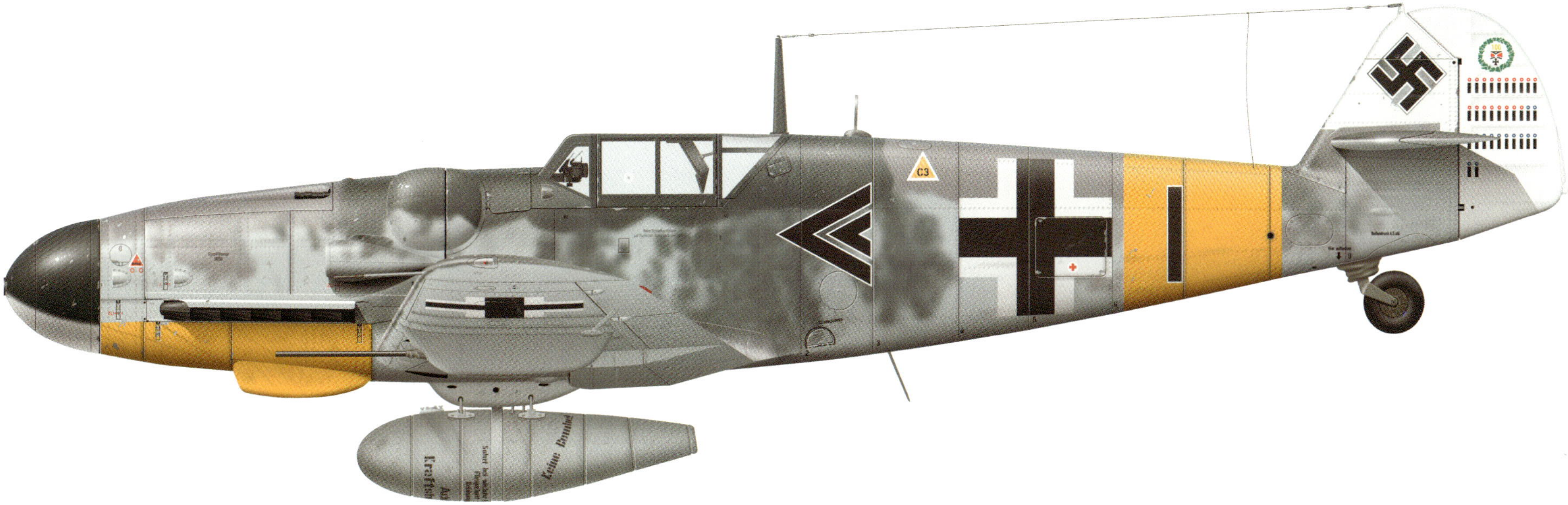
C3

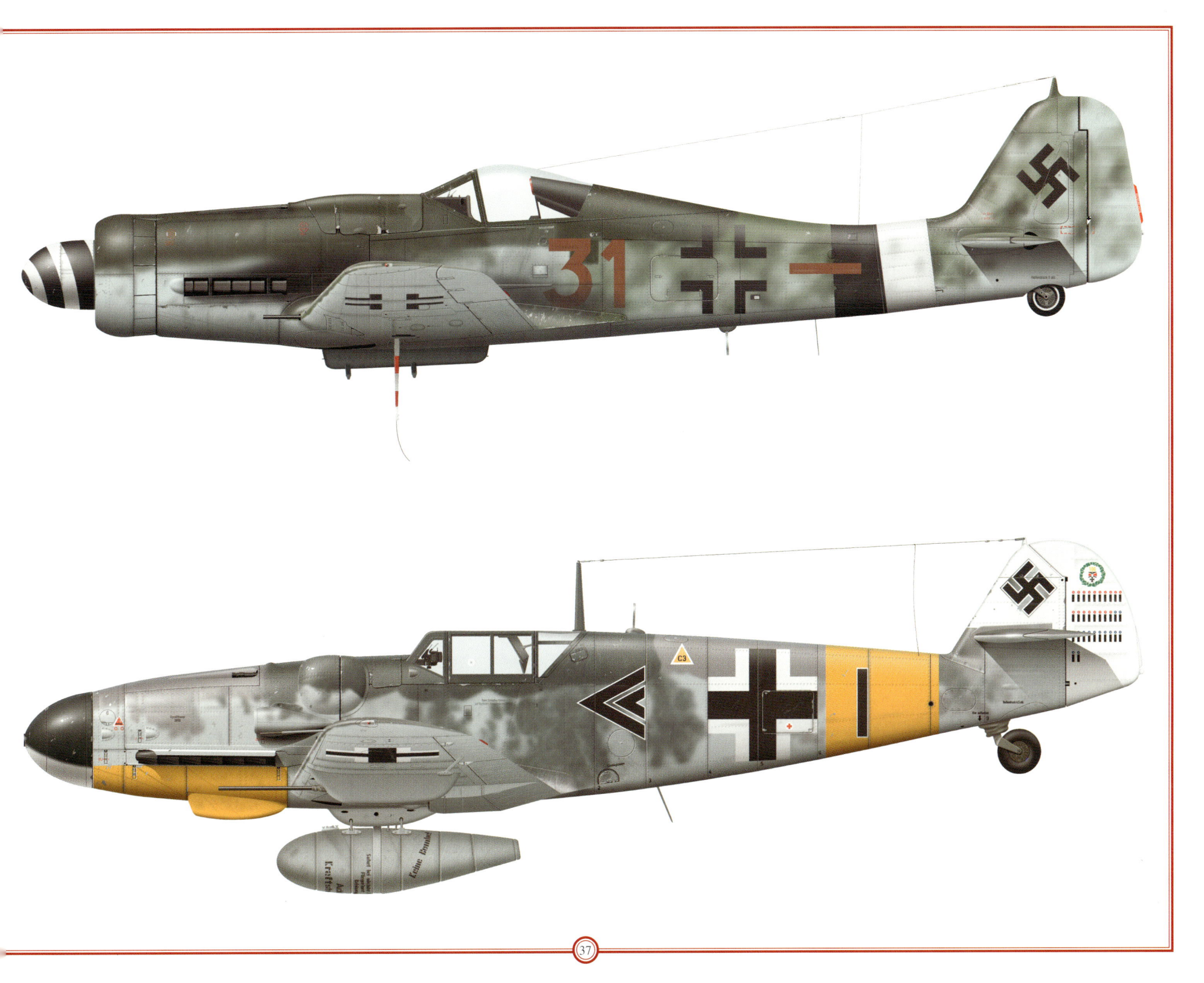

Grumman F4F-4

2nd Lt. Thomas H. Mann • VMF-121 • Guadalcanal

Notes:
Eight Japanese flag kill markings applied under canopy.

Colors:
Standard U.S. Navy two tone scheme consisting of Blue Gray over Light Gray
Prop Blades: Black with Yellow tips

References:
Marine Fighting Squadron One-Twenty-one by Thomas Doll. 1996 Squadron Signal Publications

Curtiss Hawk H81A-2 (P-40B)

Fin # P-8134
'Tex' Hill • 2nd Pursuit Squadron, American Volunteer Group (A.V.G.) • China • 1941

Notes:
The upper surface pattern was applied using rubber templates resulting in a fairly hard edged camouflage similar to RAF fighters. For their group's courage, duty, innovation, and tenacity in the face of adversity, the AVG Flying Tigers were the recipients of the National Aviation Hall of Fame's 1999 "Milton Caniff Spirit of Flight Award."

Colors:
Undersurfaces: Sky
Uppersurfaces: Dark Earth, Dark Green
Prop blades: Black with Yellow tips

References:
Original photos & interviews with Hill

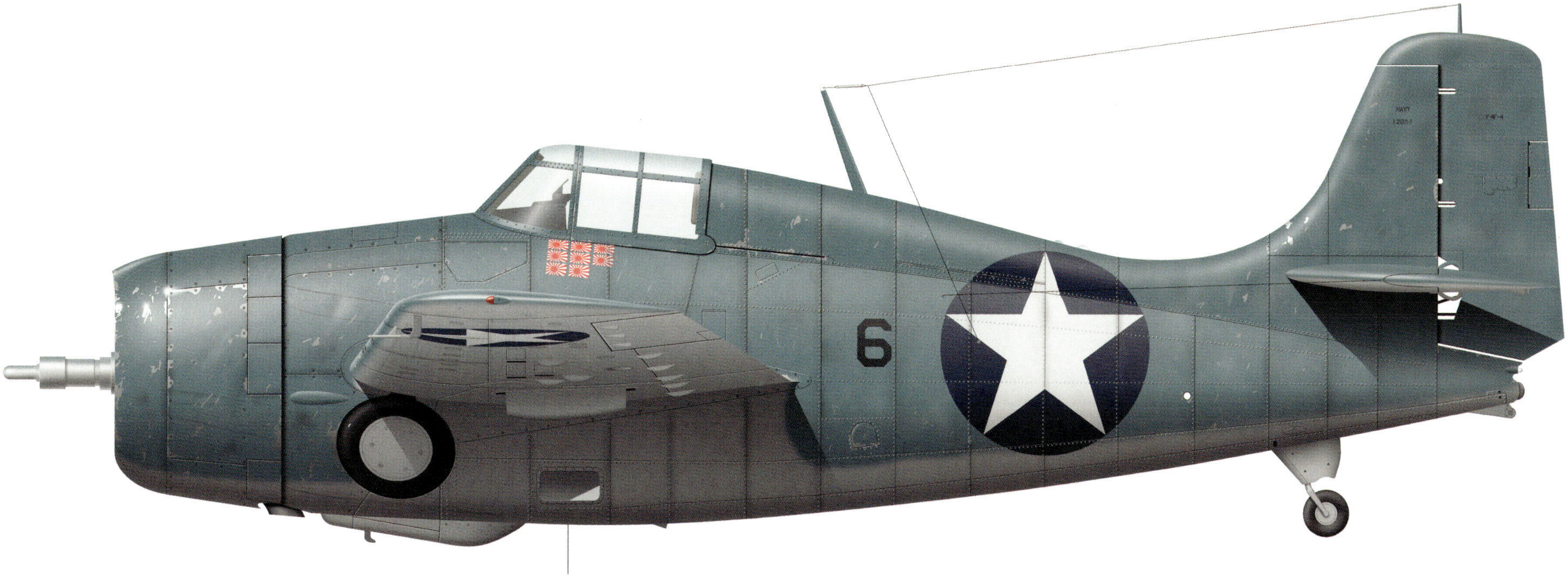
6

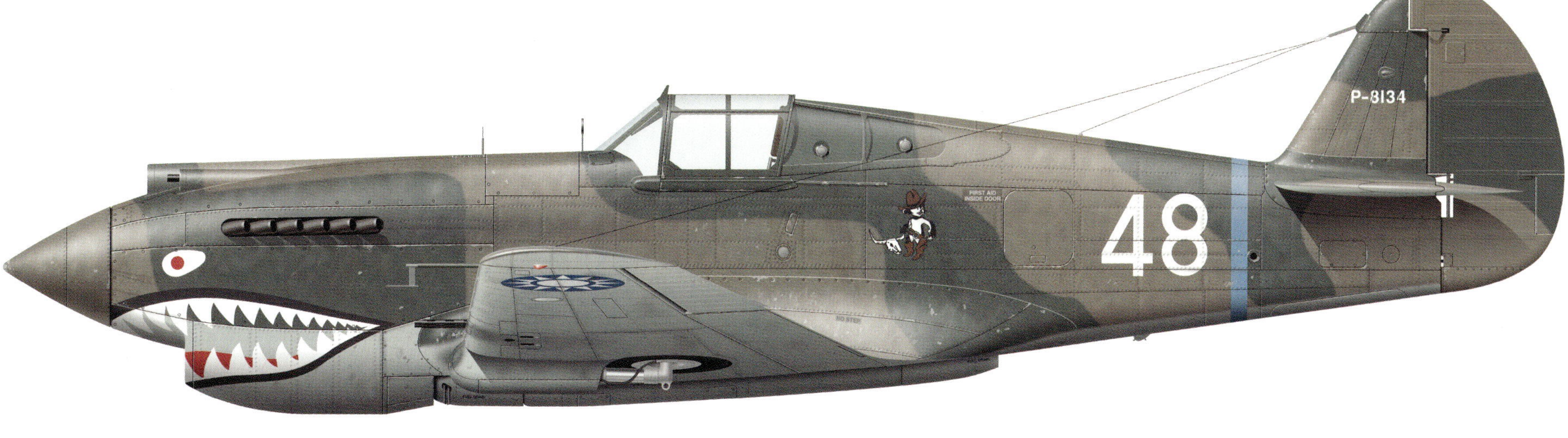
P-8134
FIRST AID
INSIDE DOOR
48

The Illustration Process

My profile and perspective illustrations are all created on an Apple Macintosh computer system using several types of illustration software. This method of illustration (generally known as electronic painting or e-painting) should not be confused with computer generated art (CGI), where a 3-D model is built with CGI software and all lighting and shadows are created by the computer. My illustrations are created using a digital pen and tablet, and are painted in exactly the same way as a conventional illustration. I began my career using a traditional airbrush and this aided greatly in my transition over to computer illustration. Perhaps the biggest advantage to using a computer for the illustration process is the extreme ease of changing the artwork as additional information becomes available. Far too often I will complete a profile only to have someone send me a new unpublished photo of the aircraft a few weeks later.

The first step in the process is to gather a reference file on the subject aircraft. Whenever possible, I obtain original factory drawings, painting manuals and stencilling instructions. If an example of the aircraft still exists somewhere, I try to make arrangements to have several rolls of film taken covering the entire aircraft and every detail that might be visible in my drawing. Once my research is completed, I begin creating my master drawing for the profile. This drawing contains all panel details, rivet placement, plus shape and contour information needed for painting the image.

Once the aircraft research has been completed, I begin selecting the camouflage and markings for the profile. Original period photos and paint chips are obtained on the subject aircraft, along with interviews of the pilot or ground crew if possible. I then make careful drawings of all markings, and add these drawings to the master profile drawing. At this stage I usually send off a copy of the drawing & markings layout to the pilot or crew members who helped research the aircraft for their input. With the completed reference file in hand, the illustration process can start.

As with a traditional airbrush illustration, the completed drawing is prepared for painting and the necessary colors for the illustration are selected/mixed prior to beginning the painting process. The second step is to create masks for any areas to be painted. Once this task is completed, the actual painting of the profile can begin. I usually start with the furthest major section from the viewer (usually the fuselage) and work forward. With a standard profile, the outline is masked off and a base color is applied with the digital airbrush. Once I am satisfied with the camouflage colors and demarcations, markings are applied, over which I add highlights and shadows in the appropriate areas. Any weathering or stress creases that need to be shown are added at this point. Finally, panel lines, fasteners and rivets are painted-perhaps the most time consuming part of the process. These same steps would then be followed for painting the wings, landing gear, ordinance, etc.

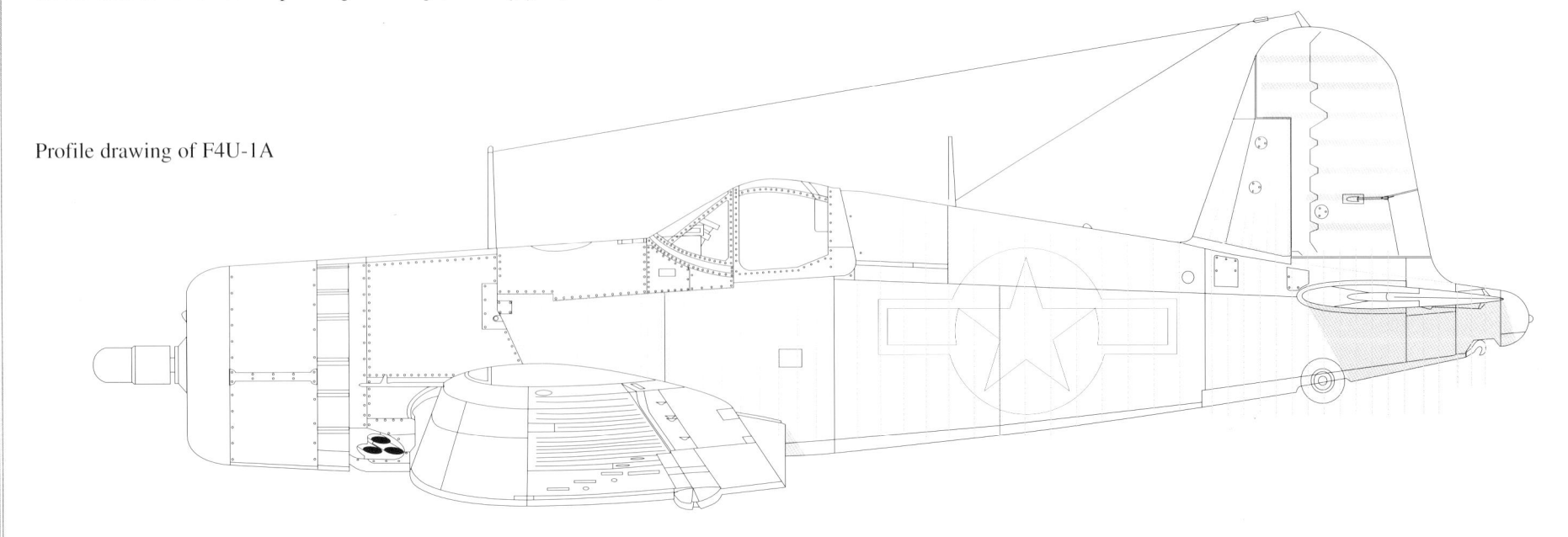

Profile drawing of F4U-1A